ILLINOIS CENTRAL COLLEGE
A12901437509

We Are All LEADERS

The Characteristics, Benefits, Behaviors and Actions of Successful Leaders

D1596627

Withdrawn

I.C.C. LIBRARY

Dr. Thomas J. Shaughnessy

HD
51
.1
.S475
1999
c.2

Copyright © 1999 by Dr. Thomas J. Shaughnessy
All rights reserved, including the right to reproduce
this book or portions thereof in any form whatsoever.

Printed in the United States of America

ISBN 0-9671818-0-1

FOR ADDITIONAL INFORMATION CONTACT:
Dr. Thomas J. Shaughnessy
Illinois Central College
Room 334B
One College Drive
East Peoria, IL 61635
(309) 694-8433

This book is dedicated to my wife Sherri;
to my son and daughter, Kelly and Robyn;
to my parents, Tom and Betty Shaughnessy;
to my brothers and sisters and to my students.
You have all given meaning and joy to my life.

CONTENTS

INTRODUCTION

In the modern business world, leadership skills are essential for <u>all</u> employees regardless of the job title they may have. Global competition and the demands of customers, both internal and external, require that all employees possess the characteristics found in outstanding leaders. Whether one is an executive, a member of a quality team, an entrepreneur, a salesperson, or the newest employee in a large corporation, leadership skills are essential to his or her success and, in turn, the success of the organization. The purpose of *We Are All Leaders* is to significantly enhance the success of both individuals and organizations by serving as a resource, identifying essential characteristics needed in today's workplace.

The characteristics essential to one's leadership success are universal. Whether the individual is the CEO of a multinational corporation or the newest employee in a small business, the qualities leading to successful leadership are basically the same.

We Are All Leaders provides its readers with three essential elements. First, a variety of *characteristics* vital to leadership success are provided. Secondly, the importance of each success-related item is illustrated through a variety of *benefits* related to each characteristic. Finally, various *behaviors and actions* identifying applications of each characteristic are presented, allowing the reader to apply more easily each success-enhancing quality to his or her career and life activities.

Millions of individuals seek to become successful leaders. *We Are All Leaders* provides a straightforward, enjoyable format leading to success. At the conclusion of each "lesson," a poem summarizes the key points presented in the lesson. *We Are All Leaders* is an extremely practical/useful tool, targeting all individuals and organizations seeking success. *We Are All Leaders* would be an ideal resource as an element of organizational employee development programs, enhancing the success of both individuals and the organization.

The setting of *We Are All Leaders* is a college course titled *Leadership 101* with a professor named Dr. Rob Kelly. The "class" meets once each week in the evening with a wide variety of students. Some are business leaders while others are salespeople, doctors, accountants, community leaders, etc., who are taking the *Leadership 101* "class" as they seek success in their lives and careers. The class has built a reputation of providing practical ideas that indeed are likely to enhance the success of those who apply the lessons to their lives and careers.

LESSON 1
Leadership 101: Orientation

"You must be having one of those Leadership 101 classes again," the secretary of the business department said to Professor Rob Kelly as he picked up his class roster on the first evening of the semester.

"Why yes, I am," said Professor Kelly, "but how did you know?"

"Oh, the usual signs," responded the secretary, "the laughter and the enthusiastic conversations that can be heard halfway down the hall."

Professor Kelly smiled. It was true. The Leadership 101 class was not your typical class, nor were the students who signed up. Professor Kelly had been teaching for a number of years when the very basic reason why students went to college occurred to him . . . they wanted to be *successful!* The more he reflected on this, the more intrigued he became with the issue of success. Over the years success became the focal point of his classes, whether he was teaching Principles of Management, Human Relations in Business, Salesmanship, or meeting with his business interns. Professor Kelly also noticed that the hundreds of guest speakers who spoke to his classes seemed to focus on certain factors, factors that related to the topic of leadership success.

Professor Kelly wanted to reach out to as many individuals as possible with the goal of increasing the level of success of all of the people he came in contact with. He decided to create a new course called Leadership 101, open to everyone with no prerequisites that might prevent someone from signing up. The first time the course was offered, the class was relatively small, but then the word spread throughout the community, then the county, until at present when there are students who drive for hours to take the Leadership 101 class. It's like Professor Kelly had always told his business students: "If you do a good job, few people will talk about it. But if you do a *great* job, your success will snowball, and your success will come relatively quickly." That must have been what happened, for every semester the Leadership 101 class was offered, the class filled up quickly. Getting into the class was kind of like trying to get tickets to a Reba McIntyre concert!

Rob Kelly walked quickly down the hall as he was always eager to meet the new students, not knowing who they would be but still knowing that they would be enthusiastic and eager to learn as much as possible about what it takes to be successful, and more importantly, eager to *apply* this knowledge to their lives and careers. As Professor Kelly arrived, the classroom suddenly grew quiet as if the students were catching their breath for what was to be the most exhilarating, practical class they had ever taken. They were right!

"Good evening, everyone, and welcome to Leadership 101." Dr. Rob Kelly could hardly contain his own enthusiasm as he gazed around the classroom, seeing the eagerness in the expressions of this particular group of students. Over the years he marveled at how each and every class had its own personality due to the unique combinations of individuals who made up the class. "As you know, each of you completed a brief survey, including your occupation, hobbies, priorities, and so on. This is essential, for I have found over the years that diversity is a key to the success of the Leadership 101 class. I am happy to report that this class is one of the most diverse groups that I have ever had the pleasure of teaching."

Professor Kelly gazed at the students, wondering which of his students were in the particular occupational categories that he knew were present in the class. He had learned a long time ago that no matter how carefully he studied the faces, he would never match the individuals to their occupations. So instead, he began to read a list of the varied backgrounds of the individuals that made up the class. And a diverse group it was. In the class this semester there were the following: a human resource manager, a disc jockey from a local radio station, a coach from a local high school, a counselor who specialized in marital problems, a computer software service specialist, an owner of a daycare, an electrician, a full-time college student, a taxi driver, a city councilman, an accountant, a lawyer, a chiropractor, a department store manager, a nurse, a retiree, a waitress, a doctor, an entrepreneur, a corporate executive, a stockbroker, a realtor, a supervisor, a pastor, a middle manager, a high school teacher, a farmer, a salesperson, a husband and wife who were also parents, a beautician, a police officer, a librarian, an architect, a secretary, and a factory worker. This indeed was one of the most diverse groups that Professor Kelly had ever had the pleasure of teaching. He knew what that meant . . . yet another highly successful Leadership101 class!

Professor Kelly went on, "As you can see, our class is extremely diverse, which I assure you will make the class enjoyable, interesting, and valuable to each of us, myself included. Let me explain the framework upon which the Leadership 101 class is based, which is one that has proven quite beneficial over the years." Professor Kelly distributed a handout of the course outline to each of the students. "As you can see, after this evening there will be fourteen sessions each Monday evening throughout the semester. On each of these evenings, we will focus on a particular characteristic that is likely to enhance the success of the individual who applies it to his or her life and career. Your assignment each week will be to research the topic and to reflect upon how the success characteristic might be of *benefit* to the individual who exhibits this trait and to make a list of *specific applications* of this characteristic to your own life and career. As we share the results of our research and reflections each week, we will be building our own guidelines that will significantly enhance our success both in our careers and our personal lives. The reason we establish the benefits of each characteristic is that understanding the importance of each trait is vital. By establishing the benefits of the characteristic, we are building a foundation for the self-discipline that is often necessary in the application phase. However, only when we apply and demonstrate the success-related characteristic do we truly attain the success that we seek. Thus, the second task is to list specific applications, that is, behaviors and actions that indicate we possess the success-related characteristic. Once we have listed the benefits and applications of each characteristic, we simply decide how to incorporate them into our own lives and careers.

Once again, a sense of quiet came over the room as both the students and Professor Kelly anticipated the results, the fruits of their labor. Professor Kelly suggested that he had two main goals for the class. One was that the class would be the most practical, useful class that the students had ever taken, and two was that the class would also be presented in a way that would be enjoyable. "You will not be a passive observer but rather an active participant in the Leadership 101 class."

The rest of the first evening was spent allowing the students to introduce themselves with particular emphasis on why each signed up for the Leadership 101 class. Although the individuals who made up the class were diverse, coming from a wide variety of interests and occupations, they all had one thing in common. They had enrolled in the class because of a strong desire to increase their level of success in both their careers and personal lives.

At the conclusion of the evening, Professor Kelly presented the class with the characteristic that they were to research and reflect upon for next week's class. "The topic for our class next week is 'The Importance of a Positive Attitude.' After doing research and reflecting on this topic, prepare the following: first, make a list of the *benefits* of a positive attitude, being as specific as possible as to why having a positive attitude is important, and second, make a list of *applications* of a positive attitude, listing the *behaviors* and *actions* that *demonstrate* that an individual indeed has a positive attitude.   Good luck. See you next week."

SUCCESS

by Dr. Thomas J. Shaughnessy
FEBRUARY 28, 1998

Success has many definitions, for each person has his own.
Some relate to groups of people, some for individuals all alone.
Some involve making lots of money or other things to do with wealth
While others involve college degrees, a diploma framed on a shelf.

Success may be the friendships that you make all through your life.
It may be the special bond shared between a husband and a wife.
The point may be a promotion, attaining a position of great power
Or simply feeling good about what you do each day . . . each hour.

Success is sometimes measured by the impact you have on others,
Whether they are employees or friends or your sisters or your brothers.
Success may be determined by the satisfaction of our customers.
Do we truly make them happy? Do they recommend us to many others?

Success has many faces, but it's something we all seek.
Whether in sports, careers, or personal lives, we all want to reach our peak.
So my wish for you, my friend, is that you become your very best,
For whatever your definition is, may you be blessed with much success.

LESSON 2
A Positive Attitude

Professor Kelly arrived a few minutes early, and all the students were already in their seats. This did not surprise Dr. Kelly, for he had become accustomed to this in the previous semesters of teaching the Leadership 101 course. This was the only course that students always arrived early for. Professor Kelly reasoned that this was because the Leadership 101 class was not a requirement and that the students were simply taking the course because they wanted to; they were doing it for themselves, much like individuals pampering themselves with a hot bath after a workout or a long day at work. The students in the Leadership 101 class were highly motivated because success was so important to them. No doubt about it, the Leadership 101 students were taking this class for themselves, to enhance their success in both their careers and personal lives.

"Our topic for this evening's session is 'The Importance of a Positive Attitude.' I hope all of you spent a good deal of time considering both the benefits of a positive attitude and specific applications of a positive attitude to your lives and careers." From the confident looks on the faces of the students, Dr. Kelly could tell that the students had done their homework in preparing for this evening's session. "I will place your ideas on the board for discussion purposes and will also develop a typed handout of your responses that I will distribute each week at the following class session," stated Professor Kelly. "Who has an idea regarding a benefit of a positive attitude in your life or career?"

Simultaneously, thirty-six hands flew up in response to Dr. Kelly's question. The first student to be recognized was a human resource manager. "I hire a great deal of employees each year, and I look for a positive attitude above all other traits."

Professor Kelly responded, "So one of the benefits of a positive attitude is that it will be of great benefit to an individual in a job interview."

Another student complained, "That's what's wrong with the hiring process. All anyone cares about is your attitude, and nobody seems to care about your knowledge and technical abilities."

The human resource manager responded, "Nothing could be further from the truth. Knowledge and abilities are vital. But that's expected if one is to be considered for any position. What I'm saying is that in today's business world, without a positive attitude, an individual doesn't stand a chance."

It had happened again! The Leadership 101 class was just getting started, and the level of enthusiasm was already reaching the point of exploding. Professor Kelly saw himself as a facilitator, trying to make sure that all students had their opportunity to speak their mind while at the same time having to make sure that the discussion focused on the topic for the evening. "Who else has a comment?" Dr. Kelly asked.

The retiree raised his hand and asked the human resource manager, "You suggested that in today's business world a positive attitude is more important than ever. Why is this the case?"

The human resource manager responded, "In the past many individuals worked independently of the other workers. In today's workplace the trend is to work in teams in which attitude and other interpersonal-related characteristics are very important. Organizations are discovering that when people work in teams, synergy occurs. By working together, people accomplish more than they can when working as individuals. You know, the whole is greater than the sum of its parts."

Professor Kelly joined in, "It's true that imagining an individual working in a team environment without having a positive attitude is hard. We have already discovered through the help of our human resource manager that a positive attitude is beneficial both in getting a job and in working successfully as a part of a team, and teams are indeed becoming more popular than ever in the workplace. Does anyone else have an idea as to another benefit of a positive attitude?"

The DJ of a local radio station raised his hand. "A positive attitude is essential in my line of work. My listeners cannot see me, but they hear my voice. It is vital that I express myself in a pleasant manner."

Using the DJ's comment as a springboard, Professor Kelly asked, "How many of you use the telephone on a regular basis?" Almost every hand in the room was raised. "You see," commented Professor Kelly, "you don't have to be a DJ on a radio station to benefit from the positive attitude that can be expressed through your voice. All of us use the telephone in a wide variety of ways, whether it is of a personal nature such as speaking to loved ones or friends or in business transactions with our clients. Either way, expressing ourselves in a positive way is important." For a few moments the room was quiet as it seemed that the students were pondering the many situations in which their voice was used to express their attitude.

The coach of a local high school softball team raised her hand. "As the saying goes, 'Attitudes are contagious.' My attitude often affects the attitude of my players. Whether my team is at a practice or in the middle of an important game, I must demonstrate a positive attitude. You see, as a coach, I try to be a positive role model for the young women whom I am fortunate to meet throughout my career. If I have a lousy attitude, how can I expect my players to be enthusiastic and confident in game situations? I am convinced that attitudes become a part of us, affecting us in other roles we play in our lives. Like I said earlier, attitudes are contagious."

One of the students who was a father chided in, "I wish all coaches had your attitude. As a parent, I realize that once our children enter the school system, the influence of the parent is extremely limited. My wife and I can preach all we want about the importance of a positive attitude, but if the teachers and coaches don't reinforce these same beliefs, the results seem rather dim."

Once again, Professor Kelly saw an opportunity to make the most of the ideas being created by his students. "In other words, in all life situations our attitudes are influential. They influence the attitudes of those around us while at the same time our attitudes affect how others perceive us. Something that will be emphasized throughout the Leadership 101 course is that we are always making an impression, whether we want to or not, so we might as well make good impressions, or better still, great ones. Speaking of which, does anyone else have another benefit of having a positive attitude to share?"

A hand flew up toward the back of the room. This student was in a middle management position for a local company. "Something that I have discovered over the years is that my attitude affects the amount of communication I receive from those around me."

"How does your attitude affect the amount of communication you receive?" inquired Professor Kelly.

"I used to have a negative, often cynical attitude," responded the manager. "My employees didn't share ideas with me very much, and this brought down the productivity of our department, especially the generation of new ideas which is very important in today's highly competitive business environment. I also noticed that I often lost my best employees to other departments."

"How did you discover that it was your attitude that was the problem?" asked one of the other students.

"When I realized that many of my best people were asking to be transferred to other departments, I decided to conduct exit interviews to determine why they were leaving. I soon discovered that my negative attitude was causing the employees to feel, 'Why bother sharing my ideas? He will just shoot them down anyway,' " added the manager.

"When I realized that my attitude was hurting the productivity of the department and making me look pretty bad in the eyes of my supervisor, I decided to make an effort to be more positive about my employees' ideas. I even began holding monthly employee recognition sessions, which were designed to acknowledge the ideas presented by employees during the month. Within a few months, the ideas started coming in, and my best employees remained with the department. The only reason they leave now is due to promotions, which I feel quite good about. I can't speak for everyone, but a positive attitude has sure made a big difference in my department."

Professor Kelly remarked, " It certainly seems that a positive attitude is especially important when an individual is in any type of leadership position, whether it is as a business manager, a parent, or a coach. These positions allow one to have a significant influence on the lives of others, and a positive attitude usually leads to a positive influence on those we come in contact with. Any other ideas regarding the importance of a positive attitude?"

A student who happened to be a counselor raised her hand. "The manager reminded me that having a positive attitude is often a good way to lower the level of stress we have."

"That sounds very interesting," said Professor Kelly. "Could you please explain how that works?"

"As the manager indicated, his negative attitude was upsetting to his employees, so much so that many of them asked for a transfer. At the same time, the productivity and idea generation of the department suffered. No matter where you work, if your productivity is down, your supervisors are going to be disappointed and probably upset. Was this the case in your department?" she asked the manager.

"My supervisor made it quite clear," the manager said, thinking back to a period of time that was pretty unpleasant, "that if the performance in my department did not improve, I would be relieved of my duties. You are correct in suggesting that the level of stress in my department and that I faced was very high."

The counselor continued, "On the other hand, when we present a positive attitude, our stress level decreases significantly. For example, in large part due to our positive attitude, the people we work with regularly tend to be more pleasant as well and are much more willing to assist us when we need help. This further reduces the job pressures and the stress we face."

Professor Kelly concluded, "Yet another benefit of having a positive attitude seems to be the reduction in the level of stress we face and an increase in the support we receive from those around us."

A man in the back of the room now had his hand in the air. "Go right ahead," said Professor Kelly to the gentleman who happened to be an executive in a relatively large corporation.

"Something that I have noticed as I have climbed the corporate ladder is that the higher the position, the less people are willing to take risks in the decisions they make. The individuals who report to me are in such high-level positions, and I have found that my attitude towards them has a significant impact."

"Could you provide us with some examples of this?" asked Dr. Kelly.

"As one moves into higher level positions, the pressures tend to increase, sometimes significantly. Many individuals take their careers too seriously, that is, they see their decisions as so important that they tend to fall into a pattern of avoiding decision making whenever possible. I have found that maintaining a positive attitude myself tends to have a calming effect on those reporting to me. I assure them that they have already proved themselves highly capable or they would not be in their present positions. I also suggest that we are all human beings, that I do not expect perfection but simply the desire to do their best, and that in the long run,

I am sure that we will do just fine. This attitude seems to have a positive impact on my associates. Many of them shared stories about having worked for highly critical supervisors who created a threatening environment in which mistakes would not be tolerated, so much so that no one wanted to do anything under such conditions of high risk."

"Thank you very much," responded Professor Kelly. "It has been said that to become great, you must be willing to take risks, and it is now obvious that a positive attitude helps create an environment that allows and even encourages individuals to take the necessary risks required if they are to progress."

Dr. Kelly now referred to the blackboard, where he had always kept track of the significant ideas that had been generated regarding the benefits of the characteristic being analyzed that evening, in this case the importance of a positive attitude. As the students focused on the blackboard, this is what they saw.

BENEFITS OF A POSITIVE ATTITUDE

- A positive attitude is beneficial in a job interview.

- In today's team-oriented workplace, a positive attitude is more important than ever.

- A positive attitude within teams creates a synergy, allowing you to accomplish more.

- Positive attitudes are beneficial in conversations, such as on the telephone.

- Since attitudes are contagious, your positive attitude often affects those around you.

- A positive attitude is beneficial in the many roles that you play in your life.

- You are always making an impression, and a positive attitude helps you make a great impression.

- A positive attitude often increases the amount of feedback that you receive from others.

- A positive attitude often increases the amount of support that you receive from others.

- Positive attitudes are especially important to anyone in a leadership position (parent, manager).

- Positive attitudes are likely to reduce your stress.

- Positive attitudes allow you to take the risks that are necessary if you are to progress.

Professor Kelly commented, "I am sure that we could continue with more ideas about the benefits of having a positive attitude. But we must now move on to our second aspect of this evening's session in which we will share examples of behaviors and actions that people with positive attitudes demonstrate while also sharing specific situations in your own lives and careers where this might take place. While understanding the benefits of a characteristic, such as having a positive attitude is important, you will increase your success only if you apply and demonstrate the characteristic in your life and career."

"Who has an example of a behavior or action demonstrating that you have a positive attitude?" Once again, many hands flew in the air. It was Professor Kelly's intention to involve everyone in the discussion, so he looked for someone who had not yet made a comment. He called on a young man who happened to be a computer software specialist.

"Much of the time, I am seeking clients who can utilize my services, and it is very important that I make a good first impression. As simple as it may seem, I have found that a smile is the most important part of my wardrobe when meeting a potential client for the first time."

Professor Kelly inquired, "Why do you think that a smile has such a positive impact?"

A lady who operated a daycare center responded, "I believe that a smile is the best way to demonstrate that you are truly happy to be of service to others. I could make a living in many other career areas, but I choose to operate a daycare because I genuinely like children and feel that since a child is a parent's most cherished possession, I am honored to be responsible for his or her well-being, and a smile helps convey this message."

A full-time college student raised her hand and stated, "I couldn't agree more. I've taken many classes, and when friends of mine ask me about which instructors to take, I always recommend those who truly love teaching. In fact, that's how I ended up taking this class because a friend of mine went on and on about how enthusiastic Professor Kelly is about his classes. By the way, will this help me get an 'A' in this class?"

Professor Kelly laughed and said, "Absolutely!"

A medical doctor raised his hand and said, "As a doctor, I always assumed that it was my technical knowledge that would be most important to my career success. While my knowledge is important, many of my patients have told me over the years that they started coming to my office because other patients had suggested that I am a doctor who truly cares about his patients and that they are comfortable communicating with me. One patient said that I am the first doctor she had gone to that smiled when greeting her. She said that most of the doctors she had been to were too serious, which gave her the idea that all they were interested in was her money. A smile really seems to indicate that you care and does seem to encourage my patients to open up to me about the problems they are having."

"I think we would all agree that a smile is a great way to demonstrate a positive attitude and is very beneficial to your success as well," stated Professor Kelly. "Does someone else have another example of a behavior or action that indicates that an individual has a positive attitude?"

A woman who had been a librarian for a number of years raised her hand. "In my many years as a librarian, it never ceases to amaze me that there are so many shy people in the world. Many people are in need of assistance but are afraid to ask for help. Perhaps they have the impression that librarians want to sit around and read all day and do not want to be disturbed. What I have found very useful is to apply the 'speak-before-being-spoken-to' method. When I see individuals who appear to be in need of assistance, rather than waiting for them to ask for help, I approach them. Once you approach individuals and pleasantly offer your assistance, it's amazing how people will open up to you. I know that those of you in the business world think you invented the concept of being proactive. Well, this librarian has been proactive for over thirty years now!"

Professor Kelly chuckled and asked, "What do the rest of you think about the idea of speaking before being spoken to?"

A student who was also a very successful entrepreneur raised his hand. "Professor Kelly, I don't know if you remember, but I took your Principles of Management class a number of years ago. I remember the session where you were comparing the level of success that managers attain to how open-minded they were. You suggested that a manager with a closed mind would surely fail and that a manager with an open mind would be fairly successful. But the manager who was 'action-minded' would attain levels of success far superior to the open-minded manager."

"What does it mean to be action-minded?" a student inquired.

"Being action-minded means that managers do not wait for their employees to approach them with an idea, but rather the manager actively seeks out employees and asks them for their ideas. This approach generates many times the information that the open-minded manager receives. As suggested earlier, this action-oriented approach can work for any individual in any position. Imagine if salespeople always waited for the customer to initiate the decision to purchase a product."

"Amen," commented a student who was a salesperson.

"So far we have discovered that a smile and being assertive in speaking to others are both ways to exhibit a positive attitude. Who has yet another idea?" asked Professor Kelly.

A man who owned a large farm raised his hand. "It seems to me that in many corporations people call each other by their last names as a sign of respect. If that works, then that's fine, but in the rural community, we are all on a first-name basis. A person's name is very important, and it just seems to make people more comfortable with you when you call them by their first name. Maybe this wouldn't work in all situations, but it sure makes the people I deal with more comfortable."

Professor Kelly suggested, "We have stumbled upon an area that is situational, meaning that it all depends on the situation and whom you are dealing with. There does seem to be a trend though in the business world where companies are finding that a more casual, relaxed atmosphere seems to open up the communication channels and makes employees feel more comfortable. Calling someone by his or her first name seems to fit well into this new casual yet professional style. Does anyone have another idea relating to how we might demonstrate a positive attitude?"

A supervisor raised his hand. "One of the things that I try to do on a regular basis is compliment my employees on the things they do well. Not only does it make them feel good about themselves but also makes them feel better about me as well as it indicates to them that I try to notice the good things they do and not just areas where they need improvement."

A secretary spoke next. "If every manager could just remember to do that, to look for the good in what his or her employees do, it would sure make the workplace a more positive place to be. It seems like all I ever hear about is the mistakes I make. I don't mind hearing about my mistakes, but it would be nice to be complemented once in a while for the things I do well."

Professor Kelly commented, "Without question, one of the best and most rewarding ways to indicate that you have a positive attitude is to praise those around you. It is very important to encourage, rather than to discourage those we deal with in our lives and careers, and a sincere compliment is one of the best ways to encourage others. Elizabeth Barrett Browning once wrote, 'I love you not only for what you are, but for what I am because of you.' " Professor Kelly added, "We should never underestimate the influence we have on those around us. Does someone else have another example of a behavior or action that indicates that we have a positive attitude?"

A man who was a factory worker suggested, "I believe that people with a positive attitude come across as confident, but not arrogant. They are happy with themselves, but they do not see themselves as above others."

"That's an excellent comment," Professor Kelly remarked. "People with a positive attitude are enjoyable to be with. They seem to be comfortable with everyone, seeing themselves as an equal to others, not better or worse than anyone else."

A man toward the front of the room who happened to be a police officer joined the discussion. "I couldn't agree more. When I approach an individual who has broken the law, I try to come across in a way that is respectful yet confident. I want the person to know that while I am enforcing the law, I am doing it for the good of everyone, including himself or herself. I can still remember being a teenager and getting my first ticket. The officer was rude to me, and I didn't like it. Like I said, I try to be assertive yet considerate of others."

Professor Kelly stated, "You are all doing an excellent job. I can see that this group is going to provide an outstanding list of both benefits and behaviors related to the success characteristics that we will discuss throughout the semester."

One of the students commented, "Professor Kelly, you have just exhibited one of the behaviors discussed, complementing those around you."

"You caught me," Professor Kelly said with a laugh. "Does anyone else have another suggestion regarding behaviors related to a positive attitude?"

A salesperson who was taking the Leadership 101 class responded,

"People with a positive attitude usually are enthusiastic. They seem full of energy, thoroughly enjoying what they are doing."

Professor Kelly remarked, "That reminds me of a taped interview of George Halas, former owner and coach of the Chicago Bears. When Mr. Halas was being interviewed, he was asked about putting in so many hours, often more than eighty each week in his work. Mr. Halas responded, 'You know, I never thought of it as work.' May the same be said of all of us. Many of us spend more time on our jobs than we do with our families. It is vital that we feel passionate about our careers and life in general."

As Professor Kelly looked at his watch he said, "Well, that's about all we have time for this evening. I hope that you have enjoyed this session as much as I have. Our topic in Leadership 101 next week is 'The Importance of Being Considerate and Caring.' Please reflect on the benefits of this characteristic as well as behaviors and actions that indicate that a person is considerate and caring. Before you leave, you may want to take a look at the excellent ideas you came up with this evening regarding the behaviors and actions that indicate that an individual has a positive attitude." The students looked at the blackboard and reviewed the following information.

BEHAVIORS / ACTIONS DEMONSTRATING A POSITIVE ATTITUDE

- A smile is the most important part of your wardrobe.
- A smile demonstrates that you are happy to be of service.
- A smile indicates that you care about others.
- Be action-minded . . . speak before being spoken to, and you will receive much more feedback.
- Calling people by their first name is often a good idea.
- Compliment others . . it builds their self-esteem.
- Be confident, but never arrogant.
- Be comfortable with others and with yourself.
- Be enthusiastic and energetic.
- Be passionate about your life and career.

THE REWARDS OF A POSITIVE ATTITUDE
by Dr. Thomas J. Shaughnessy
MARCH 8, 1998

A positive attitude will make a big difference in your job interview.
And in today's team-oriented workplace, it's a must; that is true,
For a positive attitude results in what's called synergy
As your team gets more done, having high productivity.

Attitude is also vital in conversations on the telephone,
For they influence those we converse with as we are rarely all alone.
Remember, you are always making an impression in most all situations.
So keep in mind a positive attitude sets the tone in all human relations.

When we are positive, we increase the amount of feedback we get
And enhance the support we get from others— on this you can bet.
Leaders, especially, must display a caring, positive attitude,
For their success depends on others and affects their people's mood.

Still another benefit of a good attitude is the reduction of stress,
For it allows us to take the risks we must if we want to progress.
So be polite and speak out before being spoken to,
And call others by their first name and have them do the same to you.

Be enthusiastic and energetic; be passionate about your life and career.
Be confident, but not arrogant; be honest and sincere.
So carry forth a positive attitude; you will see it's always in style.
Remembering that the most important part of your wardrobe is a smile.

LESSON 3
Being Considerate & Caring

"Good evening, everyone!" Professor Kelly said as he walked briskly into the room. He was excited, for the previous week's discussion regarding the importance of a positive attitude was excellent, and he looked for more of the same this evening and throughout the semester. "As you know, our topic for this evening in the Leadership 101 class is 'The Importance of Being Considerate and Caring.' As always, we will spend the first half of the class discussing the benefits and the second half detailing some of the behaviors and actions that are exhibited by an individual who is considerate and caring. Who would like to begin this evening's discussion?"

As usual, many hands were raised. Dr. Kelly called on a student who was a realtor. She said, "My goal is to let my clients know that I truly care about them and that I am not in real estate only to make money but to help my clients find a lifestyle that suits them. While this takes some extra time, I gain a lot of satisfaction in knowing that I have had a positive impact on the lives of my clients and their families. I have found that over a period of time, being considerate and caring also results in a good deal of word-of-mouth advertising. As one of my real estate instructors suggested, 'Don't chase the dollar. Let the dollar chase you.' "

"That sounds like excellent advice," said Professor Kelly. Does anyone else have an idea related to the benefits of being considerate and caring?"

A woman in the back of the room who happened to be a wife and mother commented, "I believe that being considerate and caring is the foundation of any long-term relationship and strengthens the bond between the individuals involved. My husband and I have discovered that a key to a happy marriage is that he focuses on my needs while I focus on his."

"Excellent advice," remarked Professor Kelly. "I'm curious. Does the class feel that the bonds would be strengthened similarly in a business situation?"

An accountant spoke up, saying, "I feel it is very important that peers care about each other at work. This is a base upon which to build a support system for each other. It makes me feel a whole lot better know-ing I can count on my supervisor and fellow employees when I'm in a bind. Yes, there needs to be a strong bond between employees, and being considerate and caring is a great way to strengthen that bond."

Before Professor Kelly even had to ask, a student who was a stock-broker said, "I'd like to expand upon the ideas already presented. In my business we earn commissions, and I've worked at previous organizations where cheating and lying were a regular occurrence. Needless to say, I left those organizations. I am happy to say that I now work in an establish-ment where people truly care about each other. This atmosphere helped not only to improve my sales figures but also to reduce the level of stress which I feel has all but disappeared."

Professor Kelly responded, "Isn't it amazing how one characteristic, such as being considerate and caring, can have such a dramatic impact on our lives and careers. One of my favorite expressions is that 'Life is not singular,' which simply suggests that one thing leads to another. When a person is being caring and considerate, many positive things are bound to happen. Who has yet another example of a benefit?"

A student who was a chiropractor commented, "It seems that I get almost all of my best ideas from either my patients or my staff. At a recent meeting I thanked the staff members for all of their help the past year and told them how much I appreciated their suggestions. My office manager commented, 'Doctor, you know that the staff is often a reflection of the doctor. We all know how much you care about your patients and your staff. Your example sets the tone of the entire office and makes us proud to be a part of such a caring practice. The patients also comment on what a friendly, caring staff we have and how we let them know how important they are to us.' "

"How true that is," replied Professor Kelly. "The most important peo-ple to any manager or business owner are the employees and the cus-tomers. Without them, there would be no business. Does anyone have another suggestion?"

A lady who was a beautician commented, "It seems these days that there isn't much customer loyalty out there. Customers will often move on to businesses who charge less money, offer a special, and so on. The best thing that seems to work for me in maintaining the loyalty of my customers is to let them know that I truly care about them. Something that I am very proud of is the fact that over ninety percent of my customers have been coming to me for years. I read somewhere that it's a lot less expensive to keep your current customers than it is to try to get new ones. I keep this in mind every day as I arrive at my salon."

"Very interesting," responded Dr. Kelly. "We might say that if we don't care about our customers, why should they care about us? Any other ideas regarding the benefits of being considerate and caring?"

A man who was an electrician said, "People are so used to being ripped off that it shocks them—pardon the pun—when you treat them in a considerate way. Many businesses make it a point to charge an outrageous minimum fee for the services that they provide. When I get to an appointment and discover that the situation is minimal, I often simply give the customer three of my business cards, tell him or her that there is no charge for today's service call, to keep me in mind for future business, and to give two of my cards to friends or relatives. You wouldn't believe how good of an investment this has turned into. My customers often remark, 'Nobody does that anymore!' I simply smile and say, 'I do,' and tell them to have a great day."

"I've got a feeling that there are thirty-six people in this room, including myself, that would love to have one of your business cards," said Professor Kelly. "Does someone else have an idea?"

The student who was an entrepreneur raised his hand. "Another benefit of being considerate and caring about others is that it significantly improves your alertness."

"Could you explain how this happens?" asked Dr. Kelly.

The entrepreneur continued, "When you are only seeing things from your own point of view, you place limits on the possibilities you come up with. For example, on a snowy day, a business person who thinks of snow as a difficulty that we must face each winter would probably think of selling items like salt, boots, winter coats, and so on. But the individual who sees snow also from a positive perspective might also sell snowmobiles, sleds, ice skates, and so on. I try to do some mental role-playing, pretending I'm a child, a senior citizen, an executive, or whatever. It's amazing how doing this increases the ideas I get. But it all begins by considering the needs of others, not simply my own."

"Mental role-playing sounds like a great idea," remarked Professor Kelly. "Any other ideas?"

A gentleman who was a pastor remarked, "I've enjoyed hearing all of your ideas. As a pastor, I am often approached by people with some pretty serious matters, ranging from marriage to divorce and from the upcoming birth of a child to the death of a loved one. Obviously, it is important that I care about these people. One of the main benefits I believe I gain from this consideration for others is that it makes me a better listener. I read somewhere that the great majority of people are poor listeners. This is unfortunate because all that is often needed by an individual is someone who will listen with compassion. As a pastor, this is essential, but I believe that all of us could become better listeners if we were more considerate of the needs of others."

"Thank you very much," said Professor Kelly. "Listening is one of the most critical tools for all of us, and I can now understand how being considerate and caring could significantly improve our listening skills."

"I would like to make a comment regarding the importance of being considerate and caring," remarked a man who was a business executive. "I have observed many individuals in their attempt to rise up the corporate ladder. Some succeed while others fail. While it takes much more than being considerate and caring to be a successful executive, the lack of these qualities is sure to eliminate an individual from being considered for a high-level position. As has been indicated by others in their remarks, caring about others is essential and leads to many positive consequences. An organization simply cannot afford to have an individual in a high-level position who lacks these characteristics."

Professor Kelly stated, "Thank you very much. It is time to move on to the second portion of our class this evening as we will list the behaviors and actions of individuals who are considerate and caring. First, let's all take a look at the many benefits you have suggested that relate to our topic for this evening." As the students looked at the blackboard where Professor Kelly had listed their ideas, this is what they saw.

BENEFITS OF BEING CONSIDERATE AND CARING

- You gain a lot of satisfaction.
- It is a great way to build world-of-mouth advertising.
- It's a foundation to any long-term relationship.
- It strengthens the bond between people.
- It serves as a base for a support system.
- It helps reduce the level of stress you face.
- It has multiple benefits . . . life is not singular.
- It is a significant part of being a positive role model.
- It lets others know they are important to us.
- It significantly improves customer loyalty.
- If you don't care about others, why should they care about you?
- It's a great investment in your future.
- It significantly improves your alertness.
- It makes you a better listener.
- It makes you more promotable.

Once the students had reviewed the list of benefits derived from being considerate and caring, Professor Kelly asked, "Is there someone who would like to begin our discussion of types of behaviors and actions exhibited by a person who is considerate and caring?"

The student who was a realtor began the discussion by saying, "I mentioned earlier that it is important to demonstrate to my clients that I really care about their needs in trying to find them just the right home for their lifestyle. One of the things I do first is to conduct what I call a lifestyle self-analysis, where I have the clients complete a form in which they rate, from one to five, factors such as closet space, distance from schools, size of yard, number of bedrooms, and many other items. Once this has been completed, I review the responses to make sure that both they and I have considered these items carefully. As I seek homes to show them, I have as much information as possible so that we are likely to find a home that will meet both their present and future needs. The bottom line is that it takes more time to do a good job for the clients, but in the long run, it is well worth it.

"Thank you," said Professor Kelly. "It seems that one way to demonstrate how much we care is to be well organized and take whatever time is required to do the job right. Are there some other suggestions?"

The beautician raised her hand and commented, "Similar to the realtor, I put in extra time. I try very hard to personalize the experience for my customers. I do this by keeping a card file on all customers, listing things like the names of their spouses and children, their hobbies, places they work, and of course, any specific comments they make about the look they are seeking. The more I know about my customers, the better job I can do for them. For example, if I know that one of my customers works out five days per week, I recommend certain conditioners that are necessary for someone who has to wash his or her hair frequently."

Professor Kelly commented, "These are excellent ideas that all of us need to apply to our lives and careers. No matter what career area you are in, you all have customers. Some of them are the external customers who purchase our services and products while others are internal customers such as our co-workers. As mentioned by the beautician, the better we get to know our customers, the better and more uniquely we are able to serve them." Dr. Kelly continued, "Too many people live and work following the 'neighborhood philosophy,' which means we only know about the superficial or obvious aspects of our customers' or co-workers' lives such as the kind of car they drive, the way they dress, and so on. Our relationships could be significantly enhanced if we dug deeper into their lives, seeking information related to their dreams, goals, and interests. This would allow us to serve their needs in a more thorough way. Who has yet another example of a behavior or action?"

The student who was a human resource manager responded, "The person who truly cares listens carefully and asks questions related to the needs of others. We have all had conversations with others in which we are discussing something that is very important to us but can tell that they are not interested as they simply nod and say 'uh huh' and look at their watch. If we are truly interested in others, we will listen actively, asking questions to help us understand them fully."

"No doubt about it," noted Dr. Kelly. "If we really care about others, we listen to them carefully and ask questions, which allows us to be of greater service to them as well. Some other ideas?"

"Consistency," said a student who was a taxi driver.

"Could you give us an example of this?" asked Professor Kelly.

"Sure. I get a lot of repeat business from people who appreciate the fact that if I tell them I will be there in ten minutes, I am there in ten minutes."

"I certainly agree with that," commented a student who was a salesperson. "In my position I deal with all kinds of customers. Something that they frequently comment on is that they want to deal with businesses that provide services and products that are consistent in quality. The business world is a tough place. You can serve the customers' needs well over and over again, but if you slip up just once, you may lose a customer forever."

A student who was also a waitress commented, "That's a great point. My regular customers often say that they can always count on the quality of our products. Whether it is our coffee or food items, people like to know that what they get today will taste the same as what they purchased five years ago."

Professor Kelly said, "Without question, something that is often lacking in the business world is consistent excellence. Continuous improvement has become the goal of many organizations and is something that we all should strive for in the priority areas of our lives both in our careers and in our personal lives. Change is good only if it means we have improved our performance. Does someone else have another recommendation?"

The man who was a first-level supervisor commented, "Something that is very important to my employees is that they can come to me and share confidential matters, knowing that I will not tell anyone unless the employee asks me to."

"Thank you," said Dr. Kelly. "A person who is caring is more likely to receive from people information that is quite personal and must, therefore, act in a trustworthy manner. Everyone has difficulties in life and needs someone to turn to, to bounce things off of every once in a while. A considerate, caring person can serve as a valuable resource to others. You may be in a position to offer such support. Let others know that you appreciate their faith in you and that you will do your best to help them in a professional manner."

A woman who was the manager of a department store said, "In all my years of managing in the retail business, something I've noticed about my best salespeople is that they are more alert than the rest. Largely due to the fact that they care so much about our customers, they seem to know just when to approach a customer and also when to leave them alone."

"How right you are," acknowledged Dr. Kelly. "People who are self-centered are so absorbed in themselves that they fail to recognize the needs of others, which severely limits their potential in both their career and personal life. If I were to ask each of you what you like most about your best friend, many of you would suggest that he or she cares a great deal about you. While we cannot be the best friend of all people we associate with, we can be considerate and caring regarding their needs. Does someone else have an idea?"

The student who was in a middle-management position raised his hand and said, "As a manager, I have found that something my employees really appreciate is my being flexible regarding their needs. For example, many of my employees are parents and have children who are involved in everything from soccer teams to dance classes. Although I can't always satisfy their wishes, if my employees would like to leave work a little early to go to their child's activity, I try to accommodate as much as possible. I have found that this flexibility actually reduces absenteeism in the long run. The more I try to do for my employees, the more they do for me."

"That's an excellent idea," commented Professor Kelly. "Many of us are in a position to assist others by being flexible. It's typically true that as you do unto others, they do unto you. Does anyone else have another comment related to the behaviors and actions of a caring individual?"

A man who was a city councilman suggested, "As a city councilman, I deal with many kinds of problems. Even though I do not know my constituents very well, I have found that if I demonstrate empathy for their needs, they are very appreciative. As was mentioned in class earlier, the selfish individual is bound for failure while the caring, other-centered person is bound for success."

"You've got my vote," Dr. Kelly said with a smile. "It's so important that we take the time to consider the needs of others, whether they are our family members, co-workers, or customers. Any other ideas?"

A woman who was an attorney commented, "I believe that keeping my clients informed is one way I show them that I care. So often I have information that my clients need, yet they would not receive it unless I shared it with them."

"That's another excellent idea," responded Professor Kelly. "Often we receive information that could be of great benefit to others. Our decision to share this information is an excellent way to indicate that we are truly concerned about their welfare. It might be something as trivial as letting them know about a new restaurant that we thought they might enjoy, or it might be a matter of extreme urgency. Either way, by passing on useful information to others, we indicate that we care about them. Does anyone have another idea?"

A husband and father raised his hand, suggesting, "Something that my wife and I have always tried to do is encourage our children by providing little rewards for outstanding achievements. For example, if one of our children gets an 'A' on an exam, we often take him or her out for pizza."

"There's nothing that works better than providing rewards to children or adults," commented Dr. Kelly. "Keep in mind that the reward does not have to cost money. I've had guest speakers in my class who give their top employee of the month their parking space. They tell me that this works especially well in January and February. Whatever the reward is, it demonstrates that you care enough to recognize their efforts."

A woman who was a nurse at a local hospital commented, "Something that my organization does for its employees to show that it cares is to pay for courses such as this one. Some gifts keep on giving, and by paying for our education, they are also enhancing the likelihood that we will attain promotions and be successful throughout our career."

"That is an excellent observation," said Dr. Kelly. "Many organizations do pay for part or all of the costs for their employees education, which creates a win-win situation, for it helps both the employee and the organization."

"Well, our time is just about up for this evening," said Professor Kelly. "Our topic for next week's Leadership 101 class is a common stumbling block that interferes with the success of many: 'The Importance of Being an Excellent Listener.' Please reflect during the week on the benefits of listening to our success and on some of the behaviors and actions of great listeners. Before you leave, take a look at the great list of ideas that you came up with this evening regarding the behaviors and actions that indicate a person is considerate and caring." The students studied the items carefully, and this is what they saw.

BEHAVIORS / ACTIONS OF CONSIDERATE, CARING PEOPLE

- Take extra time in getting to know your employees' need.
- Personalize the experience for your customers.
- Keep a card file on your clients.
- The more you know about others, the more you can help.
- You all have customers (internal and external).
- Don't follow the "neighborhood philosophy."
- People who truly care about others are good listeners.
- Most businesses lack consistent excellence.
- Change is only good if it results in improvement.
- Always act in a trustworthy manner.
- Be flexible regarding the needs of others.
- Keep the people around you well informed.
- Provide rewards to recognize excellence.
- Support the education / development of your associates.

WHY BE CONSIDERATE AND CARING?

by Dr. Thomas J. Shaughnessy
APRIL 8, 1998

"Why bother to be considerate and caring," is something one might ask.
For starters, how about the satisfaction reaped from this most pleasant task?
People will spread the word about you with stories that they'll share,
For who better to discuss than a person who truly cares?

You see, caring is a grand foundation in any relationship
As it strengthens the bond between people who share a life-long trip
We all need a support system as we strive to attain success,
And if we have others who care about us, we are indeed truly blessed.

Being considerate and caring can reduce the stress in our lives.
You see, caring reaps multiple benefits and truly helps us thrive.
What a role model we can be to be regarded as someone who cares.
It says,"You are truly important to me, and with you I will share."

In the business world, being considerate leads to customer loyalty.
Just ask, "If I don't care for them, why should they care for me?"
You might say caring is an investment in the future, for that it truly is.
The person who cares, for example, will notice things that others miss.

The considerate person is a better listener than the self-centered type
And is more promotable as well; for success this person is ripe,
For considerate people take the extra time it takes to determine others' needs.
They truly personalize their relationships; it's no wonder they succeed.

It's as though they keep a file on others to help them on their way
For the more they listen to people, the more things they too have to say.
We all have "customers" to help, some of which are called our peers.
If we care about others, who benefits most—why the person in the mirror.

By caring about others, they begin caring about you, a wonderful reward,
For we gain respect and trust and loyalty as we strive to move forward.
So keep those around you informed in ways that will help them gain success;
Being considerate and caring is so beneficial as it helps you be at your best.

LESSON 4
The Importance of Listening

"Hello, everyone," Professor Kelly said as he entered the room. "I hope everyone is charged up and ready to go. Our topic this evening is 'The Importance of Being an Excellent Listener.' As I mentioned last week, many people are poor listeners, which severely hampers their success, their productivity, and their relationships. Our goals for this evening are to create a list of the benefits of being an excellent listener as well as a list of behaviors and actions that effective listeners exhibit. Well, let's get started."

The first hand that went up on this evening was that of a high school teacher. She commented, "One of my biggest pet peeves is having to repeat myself."

"I'm sorry, but what did you say?" Dr. Kelly interrupted. Then he asked, "Could you explain why this bothers you?"

The teacher added, "For one thing, it indicates that my students have something better to do than to listen to me, so it's an insult. I guess you might say then that a benefit of effective listening is that it tells the other person that what he or she is saying is important to you."

"That is an excellent observation," added Dr. Kelly. "By listening carefully to others, whether in our personal lives or our careers, we are showing them that we value both them and their ideas and that we respect them. Does someone else have an idea relating to the benefits of effective listening?"

A retiree who was taking the Leadership 101 class suggested, "Over the years I have discovered that if I don't listen to people, they rarely speak to me. As the high school teacher indicated, it is insulting to the other person if we do not listen to him or her."

"Thank you for your ideas," commented Professor Kelly. "Let's expand on this notion. What do you think happens to an individual if he or she develops a reputation as a great listener?"

The student who was in a middle-management position said, "I'll tell you what happens. You start receiving a lot more feedback from the people around you. In my case this includes my employees, my peers, and my supervisor."

"That's right," agreed Dr. Kelly. "As an effective listener, people come to you with their ideas because they know you will listen and take their ideas seriously. What a difference this makes regarding your success."

I'd like to add a point about that," said the entrepreneur. "Over the years I've noticed that I get many great ideas from people like my customers, my employees and salespeople whom I buy products from. I have found that listening is the greatest learning tool of all. My goal is to learn at least one thing from someone I deal with each and every day. I have found that usually I gather more than one idea on a typical day."

Dr. Kelly remarked, "What a great idea—to realize that listening is such a valuable learning tool. We are surrounded by people both in our personal lives and at work. By listening effectively, we are able to enhance our lives by learning from those we associate with. Just imagine, for example, the sum of the combined experiences of everyone we deal with throughout our lives and careers. What a tremendous potential for growth if we only take the time to listen effectively! Does someone else have another benefit of effective listening to share?"

The chiropractor raised his hand and said, "As a chiropractor, I tell my patients that I am only as effective as they allow me to be. What I mean by this is that when my patients come to me with a particular problem, the first thing that I must do is find out exactly what their problem is. For example, there are many types of back pain. In order to deal with the pain effectively, I must first listen to the patient to determine things like the exact location of the pain, the length of time the pain has been present, and possible causes of the pain such as lifting a heavy object, having a fall, and so on."

"Thank you, doctor," Professor Kelly said. "What the chiropractor has just suggested is one of the most rewarding benefits of effective listening: listening improves our ability to solve problems."

"I couldn't agree more," commented a woman who was a counselor. "It is impossible to solve problems unless we first determine exactly what the problem is, what the possible causes are, and so forth."

A woman who was a salesperson suggested, "A common mistake that I see new salespeople make is that they are so excited to sell that they forget that successful salespeople need a great deal of repeat business if they are to be successful in the long run. They also fail to see that the key to repeat business is not just to sell but to make sure the products purchased by their customers are products that will satisfy their needs, which requires gathering information up front."

"Once again," commented Dr. Kelly, "we can see that effective listening is critical to our success because it greatly enhances our ability to solve problems, while also serving as an excellent learning tool."

The pastor suggested, "One of the benefits I derive from effective listening as a pastor is that it strengthens my empathy for others. Some of the things that I learn about others through discussions amaze me. How people deal with the struggles in their lives has also enhanced my belief in the goodness of people. I believe that the best way to develop empathy is to get to know people, and there is no better way to get to know people than to listen carefully to what they have to say."

"I couldn't agree more," said Dr. Kelly. "For example, I love teaching, and the only thing that I dislike about it is the fact that after getting to know and admire my students over a period of about four months, the class ends just as we are all getting to know one another. Fortunately, for most of you in your careers, your relationships with others continue for many years, and the empathy you develop for each other can become a powerful bond that increases your commitment to each other. And as we discussed in an earlier session, in today's business world we need all the support we can get."

"Using what Professor Kelly just said as a springboard, I'd like to add a comment," said a man that was in a supervisory position. "It was brought up in an earlier session that in the business world there doesn't seem to be much loyalty. I have found that listening does create a more caring atmosphere as we get to know one another and does create a bond between employees. I have had employees who have had offers to work in other departments within our company, positions where they would make more money. They've turned down the positions because they tell me that they get up every morning looking forward to coming to work, not simply because they like their job, but because they also like the people they work with, people who they have gotten to know over the years and people who will support them when they need help. My department has a very low employee- turnover rate, and I believe it is due in large part because people know and care about each other."

"We should never underestimate the power of the bond between people in our personal lives and in our careers," suggested Professor Kelly. "Does anyone have any other suggestions?"

The gentleman that was a business executive raised his hand. "I read somewhere that when employees are asked in surveys for the characteristics that they want most in their supervisor, listening is often the trait employees seek in their supervisor more than any other. I guess that says it all as far as the importance of effective listening."

"How unusual," said the counselor. "In my work with married couples, I have similarly found that the most common problem in a troubled marriage is poor communication."

"I don't think any of us need to be convinced as to the importance of effective listening to our success," said Dr. Kelly. "It's time to move on to the second half of this evening's session when I will ask you to describe behaviors exhibited by people who are effective listeners. But first, take a few minutes to review the items on the blackboard that relate to the benefits of effective listening." As the students reviewed the items on the board, this is what they saw.

BENEFITS OF EFFECTIVE LISTENING

- It indicates that others are important to you.
- It's a sign of respect for others.
- It greatly increases the feedback you receive.
- Listening is a great learning tool.
- Through listening, you enhance your life.
- Listening greatly improves problem solving.
- Listening strengthens your empathy for others.
- Listening can create powerful bonds between people.
- Listening helps create a caring atmosphere.
- Listening can help reduce employee turnover.
- Listening is what employees want most in a supervisor.
- Listening improves communication in your personal relationships.

Having given the students sufficient time to review the list of benefits of effective listening, Dr. Kelly knew that it was time to move on to the second part of the evening's session. "You came up with a wonderful list of the benefits of listening. Now let's see what ideas you have regarding the behaviors and actions of an individual who is an effective listener."

"As was mentioned earlier in the evening, asking questions is common among people who are effective listeners," said a medical doctor. "Whether my patients are children or adults, it's amazing how much more effective I can be if I create a dialogue between the patient and myself. It is also very important that I ask my nurse questions because many times the patient will share things with the nurse that they may not share with me."

Professor Kelly asked, "Is that because patients are sometimes intimidated by their doctor?"

"Yes, I believe that's true," the doctor responded.

Another hand was now in the air. "That reminds me of something," said the accountant. "So often, people have a stereotype of accountants as people who are quiet, even unfriendly. They assume accountants would rather sit around crunching numbers all day than discuss issues with their clients. Therefore, I attended a few seminars on communications skills. One of the things I remember being emphasized was the importance of looking people in the eye when listening to them."

"That's an excellent remark," said Dr. Kelly. "Making eye contact with others is important both when we are speaking and when we are listening to them. It's yet another way of letting the other person know that we respect them and take them seriously. Any other suggestions?"

The student who was a middle manager continued the conversation by adding, "It is important not only to look people in the eye but also to provide them with feedback regarding their concerns. I have found these to be the best ways to demonstrate to my employees that I am an effective listener. I do these both immediately as a part of the conversation as well as after I have gathered information related to previous discussions I have had with them. Both of these demonstrate that I take their concerns very seriously and that I will follow up to assist them in any way I can."

"Sound advice," stated Professor Kelly. "Ongoing feedback is a great way to show your support for others and to show that you don't forget about their concerns once the original conversation has ended. Any additional ideas?"

The woman who was an attorney suggested, "If you want to show your clients that you are a good listener, my advice to you is never, ever interrupt them. Let them tell you their full story, and as has been suggested, ask them questions so that you can gather all relevant information."

"I totally agree," added the man who was an executive. "As a manager, I have found that decision making is one of my primary responsibilities and that my decisions are only as good as the information upon which I base them. It is important to build what I call a support network. One way to do this is by listening carefully to others and by asking probing questions. Your decision making will be enhanced significantly through this additional information."

Professor Kelly said, "All of the ideas you are sharing are excellent. Does anyone else have another idea about the actions and behaviors of individuals who are effective listeners?"

The student who was an architect added, "In one of the earlier sessions, you discussed a style which you labeled being action-minded, where instead of waiting for others to come to you with their ideas, you go to them. It seems to me that an effective listener who was trying to build a support system would be action-minded regarding the people around them, seeking information rather than passively waiting for others to come to them."

"You are correct," said Professor Kelly. "Something that you are beginning to recognize is that many of the success characteristics we will discuss in the Leadership 101 course have multiple benefits, that is, they will help you in a wide variety of ways. This relates to the 'life-is-not-singular' concept, in which one action leads to various additional actions and responses. Similarly, one success-related characteristic can be beneficial in a variety of ways. Being action-minded is an example of this. Does someone else have yet another idea related to the behaviors and actions of effective listeners?"

The woman who was a realtor responded, "You've just helped me think of another idea. Just as effective listeners are action-minded, seeking ideas from others, I believe they are also action-oriented in that they often implement the ideas of those around them. For example, my clients share some information with me about wanting to live in a particular school district. It is important that I follow up by finding some homes for them to look at within that area. This is another way that I can show them that I not only listen to them but also use this information in searching for a home for them."

"That's a great thought," added Dr. Kelly. "Listening is only half the battle. It is also important that we use the information, whether it is in serving the needs of our clients or in making more effective decisions as the executive pointed out earlier this evening. Any other ideas?"

The woman who was a nurse suggested, "Something that I believe is very important is that an effective listener is not judgmental and is open-minded to the ideas of those he or she is listening to. For example, even though I have thousands of patients that I deal with each year, it is important to keep in mind that each person is a unique individual with personality characteristics of his or her own. As my patients share their problems and concerns, I must show them understanding through what I say, how I say it, and through my body language. It was brought up earlier, for example, that eye contact is very important. We should not judge others. We should instead show empathy as we listen carefully to them."

"Thank you very much for your observations," stated Dr. Kelly. "Does anyone else have an additional idea on our subject for this evening?"

The student who was the manager of a large department store said, "I agree that it is vital that we show our concern for others in part by listening to them. Something that I do along this line is I set aside time specifically for communication with my employees. Approximately every other month, I meet with each employee one-on-one for about thirty minutes. I call these 'employee improvement time sessions' as the main purpose of the sessions is to encourage each employee to share ideas that he or she believes will make our business better. I try not to say much but rather to spend this time listening to the ideas of the employees. I have received many excellent ideas this way. I also give employees recognition at the following store meetings, giving the employee credit for coming up with the ideas. This has given the employee morale quite a boost."

"Those are great ideas," said Dr. Kelly. "I have learned over the years that the best way to achieve something is to purposefully move in that direction. You are doing that in establishing specific sessions in which you listen to your employees. I also like the way you follow up these sessions by recognizing the employees. Any other ideas?"

The student who was a secretary suggested, "Something that I do that helps a great deal is keeping a journal. It's kind of like a diary. In the journal I record ideas that I receive from others in discussions. It's too easy to forget things unless I write them down. I try to review my journal at the end of each day with the intention of using these ideas further to improve my performance on my job or in my personal life."

"Journals are very beneficial for many individuals," stated Dr. Kelly. "In my journal I also try to record the highlights and lowlights of the day with the intention of using this information to improve. For example, if I had a great day, I try to use the journal to analyze why it was a great day so that I can have more days just like them. On the other hand, if a problem occurred, I try to similarly analyze it so that I can avoid such situations in the future. Knowing my wife was angry at me today is not very helpful. However, determining that she was angry at me because I did not kiss her goodbye can help me prevent her wrath in the future. Seriously, though, journals can be a great learning tool in which you record ideas of others. They will be amazed at how you remember things that they have shared with you.

"Well, once again we are running out of time. Thank you very much for your suggestions. Before leaving, I want to remind you that our topic for next week will be 'The Importance of Being a Person of Integrity.' See how many benefits, behaviors, and actions you can come up with that relate to the importance of being a person of integrity. As usual, take a look at the list of the behaviors and actions that you came up with that relate to being an individual who is an effective listener." Taking their time to absorb the knowledge shared this evening, the students reviewed the following items on the blackboard.

BEHAVIORS / ACTIONS OF EFFECTIVE LISTENERS

- Effective listeners ask questions.

- Effective listeners look people in the eye.

- Effective listeners provide feedback.

- You should never, ever interrupt others.

- Effective listeners make better decisions.

- Effective listeners actively seek the ideas of others.

- Effective listeners implement ideas they gather.

- Effective listeners are not judgmental.

- You should establish times specifically for communication sessions with emphasis on listening to others.

- You should recognize / reward others for their ideas.

- You should keep a journal and analyze the ideas you gather.

THE POWER OF LISTENING
by Dr. Thomas J. Shaughnessy
MARCH 9, 1998

How powerful a thing it is, this tool that we call listening,
For success is simply out of reach if this one trait is missing.
For listening says, "You're worth the time" to those whom we are with.
It's true that listening is quite valuable; its power is no myth.

What better way to learn to grow than to listen to others speak.
It's a wonderful problem-solving tool, but without it we are weak.
The feedback you'll receive is determined largely by how you listen.
Great listeners stand out in a crowd; they radiate and glisten.

It's also a sign that you truly care, that you have much empathy
You'll be much more alert and aware, for listening truly helps you see
As it strengthens your relationships, creating a positive atmosphere.
Others are drawn to you as you listen to them, for it shows you are sincere.

Employee surveys tell us they want a supervisor who will listen well.
And likewise in our personal relationships, what a story listening tells.
Do we ask questions or provide feedback to those who surround us
And look them directly in the eye? If so, give yourself an "A plus."

And never, ever interrupt others as they share their thoughts with you,
For you must first gather information before deciding what to do.
Be an active listener, seek others out in person or on the telephone,
For together we are stronger by far than those who act alone.

And implement the ideas of others, and be sure to give them recognition,
For the source is not as important as accomplishing the mission.
Keep a journal to reflect upon the ideas that you attain,
For the power of listening is magnificent, and tremendous is your gain.

LESSON 5
Integrity

"Good evening, everyone," Professor Kelly said as he walked up to the podium. "I hope you had a great week and are ready to discuss yet another characteristic that successful people often have—integrity. Integrity is one of those traits that seems to be a rare commodity in this world of ours. Business executives, religious leaders, even presidents have been embarrassed, even discharged for lack of integrity. Many believe that integrity is essential to anyone in a leadership position. I'm sure that this evening's discussion will be a lively one. Who would like to get us started?"

The student who was a stockbroker spoke first saying, "Integrity means everything to my clients. If they aren't able to trust me, they will go elsewhere. My most treasured possession is my reputation, and integrity is the foundation of my reputation."

"I agree completely," said the student who was also a lawyer. "You could have all the other characteristics related to success, but without integrity they mean very little. Unfortunately, it takes a long time to establish a reputation as a person of integrity and very little time to lose it."

The student who was also a wife and mother added, "Integrity is not only crucial to business success but also essential in a marriage. Much of the time, my husband and I are going our separate ways, but because he is a person of high integrity, I don't have to worry when he's on a business trip. In fact, integrity strengthens the love between people."

Dr. Kelly added, "There's no doubt about it; integrity is a major determining factor in our success both on the job and in our personal lives as well. Does someone have another comment related to the importance of integrity to our success?"

The human resource manager commented, "Borrowing from some of the ideas already presented, I think that an advantage of being a person of integrity is that it significantly reduces the amount of stress a person has. Just imagine, for example, if an employee lies to a customer about the ability of the product being purchased. The sale may be made at the moment, but in the long run the salesperson has lost a client."

"I agree," replied the student who was a factory worker. "When I was a young worker, I used to be afraid to admit to my supervisor that I didn't understand what he wanted me to do, and I didn't want to ask any dumb questions. I learned quickly that instead it is better to ask questions and do the job right the first time than to pretend that I know what I am doing only to make mistakes which could even cost me my job."

"Excellent ideas," said Professor Kelly. "As human beings, naturally we do not know how to do everything, and we should not be embarrassed about this. Life is an ongoing process of continuous growth and improvement. Also, as was pointed out, a major advantage of being a person of integrity is that it greatly reduces your level of stress. There is enough stress in most of our lives without adding to it by being dishonest. Does anyone have another idea?"

The student who was a business executive added, "Integrity is critical in any leadership position because leaders need to have the respect of their employees if they are to be effective. I've seen many leaders strive so hard to be popular that they actually do things that are unethical in an attempt to please others. In the long run, this strategy almost always backfires. As I said, to be most effective, leaders need the respect of their employees, who are the leaders' most important support system. It is difficult to support a leader who is not a person of integrity."

"Well said," remarked Professor Kelly. "None of us succeed on our own. We are all dependent on the support of others, and a foundation of this support system is having the respect of those around us. A lack of integrity is sure to erode this network of resources that we are so dependent on. Does anyone have an additional idea regarding the importance of integrity to our success?"

The gentleman who was a pastor commented, "I couldn't agree more that it is very beneficial to have the support and respect of others and that much of that support is dependent on our being a person of integrity. However, something that is even more important is how we feel about ourselves. I believe that self-esteem is one of our most prized possessions and that being a person of integrity has a major impact on the way we feel about ourselves. Many times others may see us as happy and successful, but we may know that the truth is another story. Being a person of high integrity goes a long way toward providing us with the confidence in ourselves we all need to be at our best."

"Thank you very much," declared Professor Kelly. "What an impact integrity has on the individual! While it is important that others believe in you, it is even more important that you believe in you. As usual, you are all doing an excellent job of reviewing the benefits of the characteristic that impacts on our success. Are there any other ideas regarding the importance of integrity?"

A student who was a nurse commented, "I believe that a benefit of being a person of integrity is that people open up to you, sharing information that can only be shared with someone you trust. In my position it is vital that my patients trust me and understand that I have their best interests in mind at all times. You would be amazed at some of the things my patients share with me that they don't share even with family members. While this can be intimidating at times, it is also encouraging to know that people trust me with such information."

"Thank you," said Dr. Kelly. "Without question, being regarded as a person of integrity will open up the lines of communication from those around you. All of us need someone we can go to with our difficulties or with matters that are personal. The person of integrity often serves as a resource to those who need someone to share these matters with. As mentioned, this can put you in a position that is quite an honor and at the same time challenging. Are there any additional ideas on our topic?"

The man who was a middle-level manager suggested, "As a manager, I believe that one of my most important obligations is to provide an excellent role model for my employees. I can think of nothing that is more vital than being a person of integrity. For example, unfortunately, it is all too common to hear about managers who are guilty of committing sexual harassment toward their employees. Imagine the impact that this might have on their employees. No matter how much the manager preaches ethical behavior, his or her actions will overshadow any such communications on the subject. We must always remember that what we do influences others more than what we say."

"Very true," remarked Professor Kelly. "Our actions do speak very loudly, and all of us serve as role models to those around us, whether we know it or not. Our actions clearly demonstrate whether or not we are a person of integrity, which leads us into our second half of this evening's session as we will discuss the behaviors and actions of a person of integrity.

Before we do this, let's take a look at the ideas you came up with as the benefits of being a person of integrity." As the students reviewed the items on the blackboard, this is what they saw.

BENEFITS OF BEING A PERSON OF INTEGRITY

- Integrity is a foundation of your reputation.
- It takes a long time to develop a good reputation.
- Integrity is essential in personal and business relationships.
- Integrity reduces your level of stress.
- Integrity is especially critical to leaders.
- Integrity improves your support from those around you.
- Integrity significantly affects your self-esteem.
- Integrity improves the feedback you receive.
- Integrity is essential in providing a positive role model to others.
- Acting with integrity is quite powerful.

The students looked carefully at the list of benefits of being a person of integrity. Unquestionably, this characteristic would be pivotal in their pursuit of success in their careers and personal lives. It was now time to share ideas regarding the behaviors and actions that a person with integrity exhibits. Professor Kelly got things rolling by saying, "As we can all see, integrity is crucial to our success, and we must indicate to others through our behaviors and actions that we are a person of integrity. Who would like to get us started by sharing an example of a behavior or action of such an individual?"

The gentleman who was the manager of a department store began, "Something that I try to discourage in my business is gossip. People who gossip, spreading rumors about others, not only create morale problems but also lose the respect of those around them. As corny as it may sound, people who have integrity either say positive things about others or say nothing at all."

Another hand flew up. This student was also a waitress. She said, "Where I work, gossip became such a problem that many of our employees quit their jobs. The owner of the restaurant created a new employee evaluation form, which now includes a category titled, 'Impact on Other Employees.' During this part of the employee evaluation interview, the owner emphasizes the importance of saying only positive things about our co-workers. Employees who gossip about others are given one warning, and if it happens again, they are dismissed. The whole work atmosphere has improved a great deal as the gossip has been greatly reduced."

"Thank you very much," responded Professor Kelly. "It seems that one of the characteristics of a person who has integrity is that he or she does not gossip but instead says only positive things about others."

Raising his hand, the student who was a human resource manager said, "I couldn't agree more. Over the years I have seen more damage done to the reputations of employees, both managers and nonmanagers, by gossip than by anything else. As was suggested, something else that people of integrity do is to build the self-esteem of others by noticing and complimenting people on their strong points. This can make all the difference in the world to an individual, especially a new employee or an individual going through a difficult time in his or her life or career."

"Thank you for your comments," said Dr. Kelly. "As we share our ideas with each other each week in the Leadership 101 class, the subject of self-esteem will come up quite often. How people feel about themselves plays a major role in their success and happiness. People of integrity can enhance the lives of those around them by their approach to sharing with others. For example, as a manager, consider the problems your employees are having as an opportunity not for discipline but rather for "corrective improvement" sessions. By the manager's placing emphasis on the fact that no one is perfect and by making adjustments, the employees can continuously improve their behavior. Remember, it's not only what we say but how we say it that can make all the difference in our relationships in both our careers and personal lives. Does anyone have another example of a behavior or action exhibited by a person of integrity?"

The student who was a father commented, "I believe that people show that they are persons of integrity by keeping their promises. Too many people say things only because they believe that is what others want to hear, having no intention of doing what they say they are going to do."

"Thank you," said Professor Kelly. "We probably all know people who promise to do things but fail to follow through and do anything about it. How do we feel about such people? Well, for one thing, we probably lose our respect for them. On the other hand, the people in our lives who keep their promises are highly regarded. Any other ideas?"

"I'd like to move in a new direction," said the student who was a police officer. "I believe that people with integrity are those who admit their own mistakes, not trying to cover them up or blame them on someone else. As a police officer, I give warnings or tickets to those who disobey traffic laws such as speeding. When I approach the people and they deny the fact that they have done anything wrong or tell me that I should be spending my time chasing the 'real criminals,' they have insulted me as well as lowered my opinion of them. On the other hand, if they remark that they were at fault and apologize for their behavior, they gain my respect."

"Excellent observation," remarked Dr. Kelly. "People with integrity freely admit their mistakes, learn from them, and move on, which is yet another way to enhance their self-esteem. Some other ideas?"

The man who was a taxi driver commented, "People of integrity treat all people with respect. Often, the people I meet are wealthy or in a high-level position. Some of these people are very nice and treat me with respect. Others, however, have an attitude that they are better than everyone else just because they are financially well off."

"No doubt about it," commented Professor Kelly. "Too many people are egotistical and conceited, which can do great damage to their relationships and their success. How much better it would be if such individuals were thankful for their good fortune, seeing themselves as no better or worse than anyone else. Any other suggestions?"

The man who was an executive continued the conversation. "Much of my success is due to the hard work of my employees, and I believe that people of integrity seek out the opinions of others, not blindly thinking that they have all the answers. Along the same line, I believe it is important to freely praise and reward those who contribute to your success. As we've discussed in our class before, success is often a result of a team effort, not simply the work of an individual."

"Thank you very much," said Dr. Kelly. "Another common theme in the Leadership 101 classes is that in order to attain our highest level of success, we must have the support of others. So much more can be accomplished by working as a team. Our class is a perfect example of that. Speaking of which, who has yet another idea relating to the behaviors and actions of a person who has integrity?"

The student who was a doctor said, "I believe that people of integrity develop a code of ethics that guides them in their career and personal life as well. It seems that individuals are continuously provided with the opportunity to be unethical, and while it is a challenge, the person of integrity meets the challenge because he or she has developed and lives by a personal code of ethics."

"Thank you," said Dr. Kelly. "It seems that in this world of ours, we are challenged ethically quite often, and if we look to the media such as television programs or movies to provide us with the guidelines to follow, we may be in for trouble. As the doctor pointed out, we must develop our own code of ethics, our beliefs about right and wrong, if we are to maintain a reputation as a person of integrity. Does someone else have an idea related to our topic for this evening?"

The student who was a realtor commented, "Even though dress codes vary a good deal from company to company, I believe that if a person is to be viewed as one of integrity, personal appearance needs to be considered. I know that my appearance has a great deal to do with the first impression that I make on potential clients. This does not mean that people need to dress formally. Their appearance should, however, represent what would be considered appropriate for their job.

"I agree," noted Dr. Kelly. "Some occupations such as a lawyer or a doctor require more formal attire than other positions, but our appearance should make a positive impression on both our customers and co-workers. Once again, we are running out of time. Our topic for next week's class is 'The Importance of Being Patient' as it relates to our success. Before leaving, please review the items you have come up with related to the behaviors and actions of a person with integrity." As the students reviewed the items on the blackboard, this is what they saw.

BEHAVIORS / ACTIONS OF PEOPLE WITH INTEGRITY

- People of integrity do not gossip.

- You should comment on the good traits of others.

- You should build the self-esteem of others.

- It's not just what you say but how you say it.

- As a person of integrity, freely admit your mistakes.

- As a person of integrity, treat all people with respect.

- Be sure to seek the advice of others.

- As a person of integrity, praise and reward others.

- As a person of integrity, have your own code of ethics.

- Always try to exhibit professional appearance.

A PERSON OF INTEGRITY
by Dr. Thomas J. Shaughnessy
MARCH 9, 1998

Many believe your most important possession is called your reputation.
What part does integrity play in this? Some say it's number one,
For it takes a great deal of time to build and little time to lose.
It's something built day by day, not something you can choose.

Integrity is especially essential to those in leadership positions.
They use it daily in influencing others and in making decisions.
Integrity helps us gain support, for it tells others a lot
About our trust and honesty; it's quite easy to spot.

While our integrity affects others, it's more important to ourselves, it seems,
For it plays a huge, gigantic part in determining our self-esteem.
Integrity determines, to a great extent, the feedback we receive.
So in the long run, it's largely responsible for the success that we achieve.

Many feel that integrity is the key factor in the role model we portray
Affecting ethical standards far into the future as well as those of today
Just ask yourself: do you encourage gossip by the way you live your life?
Do you create a pleasant atmosphere or one that's filled with strife?

People of integrity gossip about others with many things to say.
It's just that they say positive things as they go about their day.
They have a reputation of building others up in what they say and how,
To put others down, they couldn't imagine and certainly don't allow.

Admitting their mistakes is not difficult, for of themselves they are secure.
Taking calculated risks is a must as they advance in their careers.
Praising and recognizing others brings them joy and inner peace;
We need more people of integrity for what power they release.

LESSON 6
Patience

Professor Kelly walked up to the podium and said, "Well, we are now one-third of the way through the Leadership 101 class. I have been very pleased with the ideas you have come up with so far. People who understand both the benefits of various success-related characteristics and apply them through their behaviors and actions have a tremendous advantage over those who lack such knowledge. I'm excited about the ideas we can come up with during the remainder of the semester, so we may as well get started. Our topic for this evening is 'The Importance of Having Patience.' Patience is more important now than at any other time in history. This is because our world, both in our personal lives and in our careers, is moving at an increasingly fast pace. In such a world, people with patience have a number of significant advantages over others. Who has an idea as to what one of these benefits might be?"

The student who was a secretary raised her hand and said, "For one thing, I find that if I get in too big of a hurry, I make a lot of mistakes that I would not have made if I had taken my time."

"That's an excellent idea," remarked Dr. Kelly. "While it is only human to make mistakes, especially when we are trying to continuously improve, many mistakes are avoidable if we simply take the time to do the job right the first time."

The student who was a supervisor in a factory continued the conversation saying, "I agree. Often, there is a great deal of waste in the production process because people get in too big of a hurry. As a supervisor, while I encourage my employees to attain a high level of productivity, I also let my people know that quality is more important than quantity. Today's customers have high expectations, and if my company doesn't meet their needs, they will buy from a company that will."

"Thank you," said Professor Kelly. "We can see that a significant advantage of patience is that it improves our productivity, especially the quality of our performance, and as was mentioned, quality has never been as important to our customers as it is today. Does someone else have an idea related to the benefits of patience?"

The student who was a farmer raised his hand. "While I agree that it is important to produce high-quality products, I believe patience results in something even more important, and that's safety. Farming is one of the most dangerous occupations and requires long hours during the peak seasons of planting and harvesting. I have had a number of friends who have been seriously injured while they were farming. In almost every case, they told me that the injury occurred because they got in too big of a hurry. If they had been more patient, they could have prevented the accidents and injuries."

Thank you very much," said Dr. Kelly. "I could tell by the way the room got quiet that the sobering ideas just presented about the importance of patience in preventing accidents and injuries are something we can all relate to. All of us have probably made a number of mistakes due to a lack of patience. Sometimes these mistakes can be minor, but at other times they can be quite costly."

The police officer raised his hand. "The topic of patience is especially important in my line of work. There is nothing more disturbing than arriving at the site of an accident where people have been killed. I have come upon accidents where entire families have been killed or a group of teenagers have lost their lives, and so forth. Along with drinking and driving, speeding is the most common cause of such serious accidents. If everyone simply drove at the speed limit, many lives could be saved. People seem to be in too big of a hurry."

"Thank you, officer," said Dr. Kelly. "As we can see, a lack of patience can be deadly, depending upon the situation. Other situations may not result in a serious injury, but lack of patience still can prevent us from doing our best. Can anyone think of another advantage of being a person who is patient?"

The student who was an entrepreneur commented, "As a small business owner, I have one of the most significant advantages in running a successful business, and that is the generation of innovative ideas. Coming up with creative ideas that will attract new customers is vital to the success of my business. These ideas usually do not happen overnight. If I lose patience in creating such ideas, I tend to satisfice, meaning that I come up with an idea that is pretty good but that could have been a lot better if I had taken a little more time to think it through more carefully or to have done a little more research on the idea."

"Excellent thoughts," remarked Professor Kelly. "If you read about some of the greatest minds of all time, people like Albert Einstein or Thomas Edison, you realize that they often spent a great deal of time and energy in the creation of their ideas. If it takes a lot of time for people like Einstein and Edison to complete their ideas, we should expect the same to be true for the rest of us. There are reasons that it takes time to complete our ideas. It often takes time for our minds to process various pieces of information and then to assemble these bits and pieces in order to create something that is significant. Does someone have yet another idea related to the benefits of having patience?"

The student who was both a wife and a mother raised her hand and said, "I have found that when I am patient, it significantly lowers the level of stress both in my family members and in myself. As parents who care a great deal for our children, my husband and I sometimes become impatient with our children. While there is nothing wrong with setting high standards for our children, we must also realize that each person is unique and that some things take time. My husband, for example, tends to get upset when watching sports activities that our son or daughter is involved in. While the children understand that he gets this way in large part because he loves them so much, it still hurts their feelings if he criticizes their performance or compares their performance to the star athlete on their team."

Professor Kelly noticed that the room was particularly quiet, and he himself quietly reflected before saying, "It seems that we have come upon a subject that is all too familiar to many of us. Perhaps one of the primary benefits of having patience is that it can enhance the lives of those around us and our own as well. As was mentioned, having patience can significantly lower our level of stress and the stress of those around us. If we can only learn to be more patient, both with others and ourselves, our lives and careers will be more relaxed, peaceful, enjoyable, and of course, successful. Does someone have yet another idea related to the benefits of being a person who is patient?"

The student who was a middle manager commented, "I believe that a benefit of being a patient person is that it is a great learning tool."

"Could you explain how this works?" asked Dr. Kelly.

The manager stated, "When I am impatient, those that I supervise tend to be on edge, probably due to the increased stress we were just discussing. They also get in too big of a hurry because they know that I want results right away. This causes them to hurry their work, consequently with poor results. On the other hand, when I am patient, the employees take the time necessary to think things through. They also are much more likely to bounce ideas off me, knowing that I am not in a hurry and that I appreciate their efforts. I gather so many new ideas this way that I would never have received if I were expecting immediate results. It takes more time initially to work in this manner, but in the long run we are all better off, including the employees, the organization, and the customer."

"Thank you very much," said Dr. Kelly. "Are there any other ideas regarding the importance of patience?"

The student who was a salesperson said, "Borrowing from the ideas just presented regarding the importance of patience as a learning tool, I have also found that when I am patient, I use mistakes as a learning tool rather than as a cause of frustration."

"Could you provide us with an example of that?" asked Dr. Kelly.

"Sure. For example, when I first went into selling as a career, I became very frustrated when my customers did not buy my products. I became depressed and developed a negative attitude, which reduced my chances even more with my next client. Over the years, I learned to do just the opposite. If a customer chooses not to buy from me, I actually feel good because I know that I have an opportunity to become an even better, more successful salesperson. For example, if customers decide not to buy my product, I let them know that while I fully understand and am not upset, I want to use the situation as an opportunity to serve better all of my customers' needs in the future. But in order to do this, I must determine the specific reason that they have decided not to buy my product. Perhaps the reason is that I was not able to explain the specific advantages of my product over the one that they were currently using. By knowing this, I now realize that I must understand and clearly explain such advantages if my customers are going to buy my product. This leads to additional preparation on my part, making me a better salesperson than I was before and, in turn, enhancing my future success."

"What a refreshing attitude," responded Dr. Kelly. "I have told my students for years that failure is a wonderful opportunity to learn and improve, and our salesperson's story provides an excellent example of this. Success in most of our careers takes some time, and a part of this time needs to be spent examining and learning from our temporary failures. We must realize that failure is only permanent if we allow it to be so. Does anyone else have an idea related to the benefits of having patience?"

A student who was a coach of a high school softball team commented, "I believe that by having patience, we significantly improve our relations with others. Being a high school coach, I deal with young people whose range of ability varies from outstanding to quite poor. I have found, like the manager who commented earlier, that if I am patient and understanding, it takes a lot of pressure off of the young women I am coaching. At the same time, it improves my relationship with them. I try to show respect for each player, regardless of her current level of skill; and as a result, it seems that my players have more respect for me as well."

"Thank you," commented Dr. Kelly. "Without question, having patience with those around us enhances our relationship with them. While it makes us nervous to be with others who are impatient with us, it is calming to be with those who show us the patience that we all need. It usually takes time to attain a high degree of success. Let us all take this time to be patient with both others and ourselves. Even though I consider myself to be a person of patience, it's time to move on to the second half of this evening's session. But first, take the time to examine the list of ideas you came up with this evening regarding the benefits of being a person of patience." As the students quietly focused on the items written on the blackboard, this is what they saw.

BENEFITS OF BEING A PERSON WHO HAS PATIENCE

- In our fast-paced world, patience is more important than ever.
- Patience can help us eliminate many mistakes.
- Patience helps us do the job right the first time.
- Patience significantly improves quality.
- Patience significantly improves our safety both on the job and in our personal lives.
- Patience helps us be at our best.
- Patience helps us generate innovative ideas.
- Patience helps us understand the big picture.

- Patience significantly lowers our level of stress and that of those around us.
- Patience helps our lives become more relaxed, peaceful, enjoyable, and of course, successful.
- Patience is a great learning tool.
- Patience improves the feedback we receive from others.
- Patience allows us to use mistakes as tools to continuously improve our abilities.
- Patience can significantly improve our relationships.

Having given the students plenty of time to review the list of benefits of having patience, Professor Kelly remarked, "It's time to identify some of the behaviors and actions that individuals with patience exhibit. Who would like to begin?"

The electrician raised his hand and said, "People with patience take their time, not rushing through their work. In my career as an electrician, sometimes it just takes time to determine an electrical problem, but I owe it to my customer and to myself to take my time and be thorough. I also feel that in the long run I actually save time because I make fewer mistakes. Therefore, I seldom have to make additional calls because the problem was corrected the first time."

"How right you are," responded Professor Kelly. "Years ago a manager I worked for told me that there is an easy solution to every problem, but it's usually wrong. Successful people work hard and do the job right the first time. Who has another idea as to the behaviors and actions of people who have patience?"

The student who was a salesperson raised his hand, saying, "Along with taking their time and being thorough, people with patience are well prepared even before beginning their work. For example, as a salesperson, I might spend only two or three hours a day with my customers, but I often spend six to ten hours a day preparing myself for the sales presentations I will make."

"No doubt about it," agreed Dr. Kelly. "People with patience and successful people in general spend much of their time preparing. Take this class, for example. We spend only about three hours per week in the classroom but many more hours thinking about our topic for the coming week. The result is obvious; you come up with many excellent ideas each week all due to your preparation. Does someone else have an idea to share?"

The student who was a secretary remarked, "I believe that people with patience compliment others not only on the finished product but also on the effort as well. My favorite supervisors are those who notice how hard I work on an assignment and compliment me for it. This gives me the motivation to put forth my best effort as I tackle difficult assignments."

"Thank you very much," said Dr. Kelly. "Without question, many of the tasks we are asked to complete take a significant amount of time. It is important that people are recognized on a regular basis. A coach, for example, doesn't wait till the end of the season to tell his or her players that they are doing a great job. We all need recognition for both our efforts and our accomplishments. In fact, one of the leading reasons people quit their jobs is the lack of recognition for their work. Does someone have another idea related to the behaviors and actions of people with patience?"

The student who was a supervisor raised his hand and added, "The best employees I have ever supervised are those with patience. What I noticed about these individuals is that they strive to continually improve their performance but do not get frustrated if this takes time. In fact, to continually improve your current level of performance is bound to take time."

"Those are excellent observations," remarked Dr. Kelly. "It is very likely that it will take a while to improve our current level of performance. For one thing, it usually requires that we take the time to reflect upon our current productivity and the methods we use as we go about our work. Impatient people are usually in too big of a hurry to take this 'reflective improvement time' that is vital to self-improvement. Does someone have yet another idea as to the behaviors and actions of people that exhibit patience?"

The student who was a librarian commented, "As was just mentioned, while patient people take the time to reflect, leading to continuous improvement, many other individuals are in too big of a hurry. I have noticed that people with patience tend to notice this in others and encourage others to take their time and not be discouraged with their lack of progress in the short term."

"Thank you," said Professor Kelly. "People with patience tend to have above-average observational skills and are able to help those individuals who seem to be in too big of a hurry. It reminds me of the story of the tortoise and the hare or of the stereotype of men and women. According to the stereotype, men are in a hurry and often fail to read directions when putting something together such as a child's new bicycle at Christmastime. Women, on the other hand, tend to read the directions before attempting to put the item together. Who do you think has better results? It seems that it is important to be patient both with yourself and with those around you. Does someone else have another comment regarding our topic?"

The taxi driver said, "In my business, I often deal with people who are in a big hurry and seem stressed out. The people who are more patient are both more relaxed and more well-mannered. Instead of barking orders about where they want to go, they often carry on a nice conversation and don't keep telling me what a big hurry they are in. It gets frustrating knowing that the reason they are late is because they waited too long to get going, not because I don't drive fast enough."

"Ouch," said the executive. "Often I wait till the last minute before letting my secretary know that I need a report typed, a hotel reservation made, or, yes, a taxi ride to the airport. It's my fault, yet my secretary often feels most of the pressure regarding these matters."

"Thank you for your comments," remarked Dr. Kelly. "Sometimes when we are in a positions of leadership such as managers, teachers, or parents, we can place unrealistic expectations on those around us by failing to give them adequate time to finish the tasks we want completed. Does someone else have an idea?"

The student who was a human resource manager said, "One of the things I've noticed over the years about our most effective managers is that they not only have patience but also are able to turn employee mistakes into learning experiences because of their laid-back attitude. They use such situations to teach and develop their people, which not only reduces employee turnover but also creates excellent employees in the long run."

"Thank you for sharing your observations," commented Dr. Kelly. "It is true that by being patient, we can see that our perceptions of mistakes take on a whole new meaning. By reflecting on the big picture, we can see that these errors are only temporary and lead to significant improvements over a period of time."

"I'd like to comment on a behavior of an individual with patience," announced the student who was a doctor. "As a doctor, I have so many patients to see some days that I tend to get in too big of a hurry. When this happens, I ask my nurse to remind me of this because my patients' needs must come first. At any rate, it is important that I take the time to listen carefully and ask questions to determine the specific problem my patient is having."

"Thank you," said Dr. Kelly. "Yes, people with patience take the time to listen to those around them. You can imagine the results as they receive the feedback that is essential if they are to make the proper decisions. Listening is an essential skill for anyone striving to be successful, and patient people tend to be better listeners."

"Thank you for your comments," agreed Dr. Kelly. "Once again, we are running out of time and must conclude our session for this evening. Next week our topic in Leadership 101 will be 'The Importance of Having Effective Communication Skills.' Before leaving, take a few minutes and review the ideas you came up with this evening regarding the behaviors and actions of a person who exhibits patience. Thank you again for your comments." The students reviewed the items on the blackboard, and this is what they saw.

BEHAVIORS / ACTIONS OF PEOPLE WHO HAVE PATIENCE

- People with patience take their time and do it right the first time.
- People with patience take the time to prepare for their assignments.
- People with patience compliment others for their efforts, not just for completed tasks.
- People with patience assist others who are impatient.
- People with patience reflect upon their current performance, seeking to continually improve.
- People with patience encourage those who become frustrated with their assignments.
- People with patience exhibit excellent observational skills.
- People with patience act in a relaxed manner.
- People with patience exhibit good manners.
- People with patience turn mistakes into learning experiences.
- People with patience tend to be good listeners.

PATIENCE PAVES THE WAY
by Dr. Thomas J. Shaughnessy
MARCH 9, 1998

As you live in a fast-paced world, patience is more important than ever.
It can help prevent mistakes, some of which might change your life forever.
You can become more patient by trying to do things right the very first time,
Improving both quality and productivity, helping you stand out and shine.

Safety is crucial in your life both on and off the job.
By being patient you greatly reduce risks, so you can come out on top.
So if you want to do your very best, patience is required,
For it enhances your innovative thoughts so that you will be admired.

Patience suggests keeping the big picture in mind, not thinking only of today
But rather relating your future goals to what you must do along the way.
Patience is a quality that relaxes us, reducing the level of stress,
Resulting in an organized, satisfying life and leading to success.

patience is also beneficial as you try to self-improve,
As it allows you to learn more effectively, important for those on the move.
Even mistakes are seen as developmental, something from which you gain.
Patient people gradually move ahead while others simply maintain.

Our relationships are strengthened, for we don't make others nervous
In fact, we become a magnet, drawing other people to us.
It seems that people with patience are well prepared for assignments.
Clearly patience is a virtue for those trying to make refinements.

Patient people compliment effort, not only things completed,
And help others to slow down as well; life's too short to be cheated.
Those with patience enjoy the moment, taking time to smell the roses,
Seeing each moment as a treasure; patience teaches and discloses.

LESSON 7
Communication Skills

Professor Kelly walked in the room, knowing that yet another exciting session of Leadership 101 was about to begin. "Good evening, everyone. Tonight we will discuss one of the most important topics covered in the Leadership 101 course, 'Communication Skills.' Communication skills are at the heart of most of the topics that we cover in our course. For example, think about how pivotal communication skills are to the topics we have already covered such as presenting a positive attitude, showing consideration for others, being an excellent listener, and so on. Communication is truly one of the foundations of success both in our personal lives and in our careers. Who would like to get us started this evening by listing one of the benefits of possessing excellent communication skills?"

The student who was a supervisor spoke up first, saying, "One of the primary benefits of being an effective communicator is that the number of problems and mistakes you have to deal with are reduced both in number and in magnitude."

"Excellent idea," said Dr. Kelly. "Could anyone comment further on the ability of good communicators to reduce or eliminate problems?"

The department store manager commented,"In my business, it is vital that we communicate to our customers clearly, for example, about the exact days of a special sale. Otherwise, customers come in expecting a discount, and when they are told that the sale ended yesterday, they can get very upset. Frankly, I don't blame them."

The student who was a city councilman said, "I agree. If my constituents receive incorrect information about something that affects them, they get very upset, and my phone never stops ringing, which is a giant headache for my staff and me."

"Thank you," Dr. Kelly continued. "As we can all see, miscommunication creates problems for both the intended receiver of the communication and the communicator as well. The reduction and elimination of problems are two key benefits of excellent communication skills. Could someone else share yet another benefit?"

The young man who was a computer software service specialist said,

"When I get called in to work on a big project for a company, typically I am a member of a project team. What stands out most in terms of the benefits of communication skills in this situation is that productivity soars when the team facilitator is an effective communicator. But if the facilitator lacks effective communication skills, the productivity is poor."

"Thank you," said Dr. Kelly. "From a business perspective, another of the most significant benefits of effective communication is that it enhances productivity dramatically. Before individuals or teams can complete a task, they must first have a clear understanding of what their objective is. Does someone else have another significant benefit related to effective communication skills?"

The student who was an executive suggested that "Unless an individual has excellent communication skills, he or she has little or no chance of attaining a leadership position. Leaders spend more time in communication-related activities than anything else. Moreover, the further one moves up the organizational ladder, the more important communication skills are as the individual not only communicates to more people within the organization but also spends more time communicating with those outside the organization. As stated earlier by Professor Kelly, communication skills are truly an important part of the foundation for success."

"Thank you," said Dr. Kelly. "As you can see, while communication skills are important to all of us, they become even more essential as individuals move into positions of responsibility both in their career as well as in their personal lives. Consider, for example, the importance of communication to parents, community leaders, and so on. Does someone else have a suggestion related to the benefits of effective communication skills?"

The student who was a nurse commented, "In our medical practice, communication skills are vital for many reasons. For example, it is natural for our patients to be somewhat apprehensive when they come to our office, particularly if they have a serious health problem. Our staff, including the receptionist, the nurses, and the doctor, must all be effective communicators if we are to create a comfortable relationship with our patients. In listening to our patients, I often hear more about how the patients appreciate our warm, friendly atmosphere than about the actual treatment the patients receive. In fact, I believe that by communicating effectively with the patients and getting them to relax, we are lowering their level of stress and helping to ensure that the patients will return again in the future for other medical needs."

"Thank you," remarked Professor Kelly. "Without question, communication skills are essential in establishing and maintaining long-term relationships with others. It is only in communicating that we can truly get to know one another and begin to care for those same individuals. Does anyone have yet another benefit of effective communication skills to add?"

The full-time college student raised his hand. "Over the years I have had quite a number of instructors. One of the most important factors that seems to separate the excellent teachers from the rest is how clearly they communicate the material to the students. Some instructors are brilliant, yet they cannot communicate in a way that allows the students to understand the subject matter. So I would have to say that a key benefit of effective communication skills is that the receiver of the message understands exactly what the speaker wishes to communicate."

"Excellent observation," said Dr. Kelly. "We can possess wonderful ideas, but if we cannot present them in such a way that others understand and can thus apply this information, it does little good, and in fact, leads to frustration. Does everyone understand what I just said, or do I need to repeat myself?" Professor Kelly asked jokingly. "Who else has an idea related to the benefits of having excellent communication skills?"

The student who was an entrepreneur commented, "I have noticed that the better my managers communicate, the faster our employees develop. Communication skills are essential to the continuous improvement of both the employees and the organization as well."

"You are so right," added Dr. Kelly. "Often the development of employees in businesses or children in families is dependent on the communication skills of the managers or parents, respectively. This is one of the primary reasons that we should all continue to improve our communication skills, for these skills ensure that our impact on those around us will be a more positive one. Any other ideas?"

The student who was also a high school softball coach added, "I believe that if leaders of any kind are to have the respect of their employees, players, or children, they must be able to communicate effectively. As was mentioned earlier, leaders spend more time in communication-related activities than anything else. Whether we know it or not, we are always making an impression on those around us. In my case, it's the players, the parents, the fans, the umpires, and so forth. I believe that the most important ingredient of the impression I make is through effective communication skills."

"Thank you," said Dr. Kelly. "I agree with you that our ability to communicate plays a key role in our receiving respect from those around us and in making an impression on these same individuals. It's almost time to move on to the second part of this evening's session. I'd like to close this segment by suggesting that effective communication skills enhance every aspect of our careers and personal lives. We should never stop trying to improve further this vital element as we strive to become successful. Before moving on to the second half of this evening's session, please take a few minutes to review the suggestions you shared this evening regarding the benefits of having effective communication skills." As the students reviewed the list of ideas on the board, this is what they saw.

BENEFITS OF HAVING EFFECTIVE COMMUNICATION SKILLS

- The number of problems you face decreases.
- Effective communication enhances productivity.
- Communication improves the likelihood of getting a promotion.
- Communication helps reduce the stress in the communicator's work area.
- Communication helps establish and maintain relationships.
- Understanding is significantly improved.
- Communication is essential to the continuous improvement of people and organizations.
- It enhances the respect of the communicator.
- It positively affects every aspect of one's career and personal life.

Professor Kelly began the second half of the evening's discussion by saying, "It is obvious that effective communication skills are vital to an individual's quest for success. Now it is time to identify the behaviors and actions of individuals that demonstrate their effectiveness regarding communication skills. Who would like to get us started?"

The student who was a salesperson began, "One of the most important indicators of one's ability to communicate effectively is the ability to speak clearly so that the receiver of the message fully understands."

"Thank you," said Dr. Kelly. "Could you provide us with an example of this?"

The salesperson said, "When I am trying to persuade a potential customer to buy one of my products, it is vital that I clearly explain each of the benefits of the product. This builds the value of the product in the customer's eyes. Without a clear understanding of such benefits, the sale will not be made."

"Thank you," said Dr. Kelly. "There is no doubt that the ability to convey clearly the message to others is an excellent way to demonstrate our ability to communicate effectively. Does someone else have another idea?"

The student who was also an accountant suggested, "When I am assisting a client, it is important that I explain the purpose of my recommendation from his or her point of view. My clients are interested in what I have to say that will benefit them, so I focus my remarks on how what I have to say will be beneficial to them."

"Thank you," concurred Professor Kelly. "When speaking to others, we must communicate in a way that creates an interest on their part. Once they realize that our comments are beneficial to their needs and wants, we have created an interest on their part which makes our communication much more effective. Could someone share yet another idea?"

The student who was a lawyer commented, "I have found that it is important to use language that my clients can easily understand. It is ineffective to use big words that have little or no meaning to others, and, in fact, it often irritates them if I do so. I guess this relates to what we were discussing earlier about speaking clearly and being understood. I have discovered that in my profession it is important to utilize a vocabulary that allows you to use words that the receiver of the message understands, while at the same time indicating that you are knowledgeable about your subject."

"Thank you," responded Dr. Kelly. "Without question, the words used should be selected after considering the individual we are speaking to. Are there some other ideas related to effective communication skills?"

The student who was a middle manager said, "I attend quite a few seminars, many of which last several days. Something that I have noticed is that the most effective speakers are enthusiastic about their subject matter. The way I look at it is if they aren't passionate about their subject matter, then why should I be?"

"Well said," commented Dr. Kelly. "It is very important that we believe in what we say, and this message should come across loud and clear to our audience. This is true whether we are a parent, a teacher, a pastor, or a business leader. Who has yet another idea that they strongly believe in?"

The student who was a factory worker said, "I agree with everything that is being said about effective communicators being excellent speakers. On the other hand, I believe that great communicators are also excellent listeners. If my supervisor listens to me when I have a comment to make, I am much more likely to listen to him when he speaks to me."

"Thank you," said Dr. Kelly. "It's true that by listening effectively to others, we significantly increase the likelihood that they will, in turn, listen to us when we wish to speak. Does someone else have an idea?"

The student who was also a chiropractor commented, "Along with effective communicators being good listeners, I believe that to demonstrate effectiveness in our communications, we need also to encourage feedback from others. In my position, before I can effectively treat a patient, I first ask a number of questions. Once the patient answers each question, I often seek additional information about certain areas of importance. This shows my patients that I want to do my very best for them and allows me to provide the most effective services for them."

"Thank you," remarked Professor Kelly. "Effective communicators seek feedback from those around them. As was suggested, this feedback is useful in making decisions in solving problems, providing suggestions, and so forth. Who else has another suggestion?"

The student who was a librarian said, "I believe that effective communicators get right to the point. Sometimes we can get confused because the individual talks about so many topics that we are not sure what he or she wants to tell us."

"That's a good idea," said Dr. Kelly. "Effective communicators typically get right to the point so that the receiver understands exactly what the issue is. Once again, you are doing an excellent job in identifying behaviors and actions of successful individuals. Does someone have yet another idea?"

The student who was a business executive said, "Effective communicators often use examples to clarify their message. It is often difficult to help the receivers of the message understand what we are asking them to do, so providing examples to illustrate exactly what we are asking them to accomplish is beneficial."

"Thank you," noted Dr. Kelly. "Great communicators often provide examples. In many of the best textbooks that I have used, the author provides examples to help the student comprehend the subject matter. Leaders can do the same thing when they are explaining a task to an employee or when parents are explaining a chore to one of their children. Can anyone else think of an example of a behavior or action often used by effective communicators?"

The student who was a realtor commented, "I believe that it is important to maintain good eye contact, whether you are listening to others or speaking to them. It indicates interest in them as well as respect."

"Thank you," said Dr. Kelly. "Eye contact is very important in communications. As mentioned, it doesn't matter if you are speaking or listening, eye contact is a great way to say, 'I'm interested in what you are saying' or 'I'm eager to assist you in any way that I can.' Are there any other ideas related to our topic that haven't yet been mentioned?"

The student who was a supervisor said, "Effective communicators use a variety of methods when communicating. Sometimes the telephone is effective while other situations call for face-to-face meetings, a written message, and so on."

"Good ideas," said Professor Kelly. "Those of us who are able to use various methods of communication effectively have a definite advantage over those who always rely on the same technique. We should always consider factors such as the importance of the message, the receiver of the audience, the amount of time we have to communicate, and so forth. Any other ideas?"

The student who was a stockbroker commented, "If the message is detailed or lengthy, I think it's important to provide an introduction and a summary, indicating the key points that make up the message."

"Thank you," replied Dr. Kelly. "Sometimes our message is lengthy or includes many details, and it requires that we repeat the key points a number of times. By providing an introduction and a summary, we are able to highlight these points so that the listener can focus on the important matters. Thank you very much for all of your ideas, but as usual, we are about to run out of time. Our topic for next week's class is 'The Importance of Praising and Recognizing Others' and how this relates to our success. Before you leave, please take a look at the many ideas you have provided which relate to the behaviors and actions of an effective communicator." As the students scanned the items on the board, this is what they observed.

BEHAVIORS / ACTIONS OF EFFECTIVE COMMUNICATORS

- Effective communicators speak clearly and thus are easily understood.
- Effective communicators explain the purpose of their message.
- Effective communicators use an appropriate vocabulary.
- Effective communicators are enthusiastic.
- Effective communicators are good listeners.
- Effective communicators encourage feedback.
- Effective communicators get right to the point.
- Effective communicators use practical examples.
- Effective communicators maintain good eye contact.
- Effective communicators use a variety of methods.
- Effective communicators use an introduction and a summary.

COMMUNICATION SKILLS
by Dr. Thomas J. Shaughnessy
MARCH 9, 1998

Communicating is what people do most along the way.
Effective communication skills will reduce the problems faced today,
And they set the tone for the future as well, boosting productivity.
Through effective communications we create team unity.

Good communicators are much more likely to receive a promotion.
Communication is what sets the entire organization in motion.
By communicating clearly, others are less confused,
For they know their true purpose, feeling important, not misused.

Communications are vital in building strong relationships among peers
So that a bond is formed among them that will last for many years.
Perhaps most importantly, understanding is significantly increased,
Leading to continuous improvement as communication's power is released.

Those who communicate effectively build a great reputation
And are likely to excel in their interpersonal relations.
It's hard to imagine an aspect of life not improved.
Through effective communications, many problems are removed.

Through clear communications, the person is easily understood,
And the gist of his or her message comes across quite good.
Often the communicator gets right to the key issue,
Using practical examples to make sure the point gets through.

Good eye contact and gestures are but a few of the tools
That make communicators effective, for they follow all the rules,
Using a variety of methods and various styles that are stressed,
Knowing that communications skills are a major factor in their success.

LESSON 8
Praise and Recognition

As Professor Kelly walked into the room, he knew that he and the students were in for a special session. "Good evening, everyone. Tonight our topic is 'The Importance of Praising and Providing Recognition to Others.' We are now approximately half way through the Leadership 101 course. I have been very pleased with your participation so far and am eager to find out what you have come up with regarding the importance of praising and recognizing others and specific actions and behaviors of people who have mastered these important abilities. Let's begin by analyzing the benefits of giving praise and recognition to others. Who has an idea?"

The student who was a D.J. on a radio station responded, "Over the years I have had the opportunity to meet many people. One of the things that I have learned is that when you praise others, you build their self-esteem and thus open up many possibilities for them that would not be achievable without this feeling of self- confidence."

"Thank you very much," said Professor Kelly. "It's true that self-esteem and self-confidence can make all the difference in people's success and that one of the best ways to boost others' self-esteem is to praise them for something that you admire them for. While self-esteem is often the starting point of success, praise and recognition are the building blocks of self-esteem. Does someone have another benefit of praising and recognizing the good in others?"

The student who was an entrepreneur commented, "Sincere praise and recognition are the best ways I know to increase the productivity of my employees. Over the years I have given my employees a number of surveys regarding job satisfaction. Typically, receiving praise and recognition for their efforts ranks number one."

"No doubt about the fact that praise and recognition are important to employees in all positions," added Dr. Kelly. "In fact, the number one reason employees leave a job is the lack of recognition for their efforts. As we can already see, giving praise and recognition to those around us is very important. Does someone have another idea as to the benefits of giving praise and recognition?"

The student who was a human resource manager said, "I have seen many managers come and go over the years. Something that I've been made keenly aware of is the importance of the employees having respect for their supervisor. One of the best ways to earn the respect of your employees is to recognize their performance. This does not mean that leaders should go around saying 'good job' when they talk to their employees. Instead, it is vital that leaders praise their employees by bringing up specific situations deserving recognition. This type of praise not only makes the employees feel good about themselves but also indicates that the supervisor makes it a point to observe and recognize good work and that the leader respects the work of the employees. In turn, this is one of the best ways for leaders to earn the respect of their employees."

"Excellent remarks," said Dr. Kelly. "Whether we are leaders in a business setting or parents in a home, praising for specific good deeds tells others that they are important to us and that we appreciate them. This results in a relationship that is stronger and largely based on mutual respect. Does someone else have an idea to add?"

The student who was a father suggested, "As a parent, I have always felt that the best way to develop my children is to serve as a positive role model. If my children observe me praising others, including themselves, they are much more likely to do the same with the people around them. While it is important to value yourself, I believe that it is just as important to value others, and I am sure that those with the gift of sincere praise are well on their way to successful relationships with others."

"Thank you very much," replied Dr. Kelly. "You have presented us with two important benefits of praising others. First of all, by praising others, we teach those around us to do likewise in their lives and careers. At the same time, we have helped those same individuals improve in their relationships with others. Earlier, the concept of self-esteem was discussed. By praising others and thus helping them find success in their own lives, we certainly have done something to feel good about. Does anyone have another idea related to the benefits of praising and recognizing others?"

The full-time college student raised his hand and said, "I know that we have already brought up the idea that through praising we improve the productivity of those we recognize, but I'd like to add something to this issue. I believe that by recognizing the good work of others, we encourage them to go beyond our expectations to achieve extraordinary results."

"Good point," said Professor Kelly. "It's amazing when you consider the power of sincere praise. When you think of some of the greatest coaches of all time, many of them had the gift of encouraging their players through praise, helping them achieve feats that would have otherwise seemed impossible. Think about your favorite supervisor of all the jobs you have ever had. One of the things that probably stands out about him or her is that he or she encouraged you by praising and recognizing you. And how did you respond? Hopefully, by doing your best. Praise helps ordinary people do extraordinary things. Who has yet another idea?"

The student who was a factory supervisor said, "One of the main benefits of praising others is that it raises the morale and creates a much more positive work atmosphere. As mentioned earlier, the praise must be honest and sincere, or it will do more harm than good. All of us need recognition. I try to let my employees know when they are doing a good job, and they really appreciate the fact that I notice their efforts and that I take the time to let them know how pleased I am with their efforts."

"Thank you very much," said Dr. Kelly. "We all know how important it is to have a positive work environment. One of the best ways to create such an environment is by recognizing the value of those around us. While it is important for supervisors to praise their employees, it is similarly important for the employees to let their supervisors know that they also appreciate their efforts. As we discussed earlier, we all need praise and recognition. I believe we have time for one more idea if anyone has one."

The student who was a retiree commented, "Over my career, I worked for many different organizations. Something that I noticed was that while some organizations had a great deal of employee turnover, others did not have this problem. Although there were a number of factors involved, one of the most important factors was related to praise and recognition. People do not want to work somewhere when the only time their name is mentioned is when they've done something wrong. I worked at a few places like that, but not for long. I don't mind being told about an area that I need to improve on, but I do mind if I never hear anything good about my work."

"Thank you," responded Dr. Kelly. "From a business point of view, employee turnover can be a major problem and a costly one. While other factors can be to blame, we can certainly reduce our employee turnover by providing our employees with some well-deserved praise and recognition. As you can see, there are many benefits of praising and recognizing others. Before we move on to the second segment of this evening's session, take a look at the items on the blackboard regarding the benefits of praising and recognizing others." As the students studied the items on the board, this is what they saw.

BENEFITS OF PRAISE AND RECOGNITION

- Praise builds the self-esteem of others.
- Sincere praise increases employee productivity.
- Praise and recognition are very important to employees.
- Leaders who recognize others earn their respect.
- Praise and recognition help show appreciation.
- Praising is a great way for someone to be a positive role model.
- Praising significantly improves relationships.
- Praise helps ordinary people do extraordinary things.
- Praise helps create a positive work atmosphere.
- Praise helps reduce employee turnover.

Professor Kelly began the second half of the evening's session by saying, "Now that we have listed the many benefits of praising and recognizing others, it's time to list the actions and behaviors of individuals who are effective when it comes to praising and recognizing those around them. Who would like to get us started with an idea?"

The student who was a pastor raised his hand and suggested, "I believe that people who are effective in praising others illustrate praise not only by what they say but also by how they look and act. These individuals are truly happy for the successes of others. It is all too common to find jealousy and envy in others when we find some measure of success.

What a wonderful quality it is to be truly happy for those around us who find good fortune, whether it is in having a baby, getting a promotion at work, or being blessed with financial gain."

"Thank you," said Dr. Kelly. "We are all aware of how important non-verbal communication is. Individuals who are effective in giving praise express it not only in their words but also in their eyes and facial expressions as well. Does someone else have an idea?"

The student who was a waitress commented, "In the business world, the supervisors who are effective when providing recognition for their employees use a variety of techniques. Sometimes they give you a bonus or other form of cash reward while other times they give you a day off to show appreciation for your hard work. I like surprises, so not knowing how I'm going to be rewarded is exciting."

"Thank you for your ideas," continued Dr. Kelly. "It's true that there are many ways to recognize those around us. In fact, when we use a variety of methods to praise others, it demonstrates how much we appreciate them and that we are willing to put forth an effort ourselves in coming up with a variety of ways to recognize them. Does anyone have something else to share on our topic?"

The student who operated a daycare center said, "Something that I always tell my employees is to be very specific when praising others, especially the young children that we are responsible for. If we tell children that we are proud of them because they were very well-behaved that day, children may not understand what it was that they had done. On the other hand, if we let them know that we are proud of the fact that they shared their crayons with another child, we teach them that sharing is very important in our relationships with others."

"Excellent idea," said Professor Kelly. "One of the best ways we can let others know that our praise is sincere is to explain specifically what it was that they did to earn our praise. This works not only with young children but also with adults. As mentioned, by being specific we are also using recognition as a developmental tool. Does someone else have an idea that involves the behaviors and actions of individuals who use praise and recognition effectively?"

The student who was an executive commented, "In a business, I believe it is very important to relate the praise to the success of the organization so that the individual understands how important he or she is to the business. People who realize that their efforts are a part of their organization's success feel better about themselves and about the organization as a whole."

"Thank you," said Dr. Kelly. "Many people have no idea as to how they fit into the big picture, whether we are talking about the success of a family or a business. We need to make an effort to express relationships when we praise. Many wonderful people have no idea as to how important they really are. People who are effective when it comes to praising and recognizing others often help those around them realize their value. As you can see, sincere praise can have a very positive impact on the lives of others. Does someone else have an idea that they would like to share?"

The student who was a middle manager said, "We all know how important it is to discipline an employee in private. When it comes to praising and recognizing employees, the opposite is usually true. Praise is such a positive experience that it is even more special if it occurs with others around such as fellow employees. In fact, when managers praise in public, additional praise is often given to the employees by those present at the initial recognition ceremony."

"Thank you," agreed Dr. Kelly. "It's true that most people like to be praised in public. Think of how empty graduation ceremonies or weddings would be if no one was invited to share in the joy of the event. In fact, those who care about the people involved also get a feeling of satisfaction. Similarly, when we praise in public, many of the individuals who witness the recognition benefit from the experience as well. Does anyone else have an idea to share?"

The student who was a salesperson suggested, "In addition to the enjoyment that others get from being a part of the public praising, effective individuals praise in public in order to improve further the performance of those involved. For example, when I attend a recognition ceremony of any kind, I gather ideas that may be applied to my own career, helping me as I try to continually improve my own performance."

"Thank you very much," said Dr. Kelly. "Successful people realize that most success-related characteristics may be universally applied. For example, being an effective communicator is beneficial to anyone. When people conduct the praising in public, those attending can benefit by discovering what made the individual worthy of such recognition and by applying it to their own lives and careers. Any other ideas?"

The student who was a manager of a department store said, "People who are effective when it comes to praising are alert and pay special attention to initiative demonstrated by their employees. This means that they are aware of each individual's responsibilities and take the time to praise the employee for demonstrating initiative or going beyond his or her normal duties."

Thank you very much," said Dr. Kelly. "It seems that supervisors who are effective at praising and recognizing their employees are knowledgeable regarding employee duties and are alert enough to notice when employees go beyond expectations. By doing this, they encourage both the employees and their peers to continually improve their performance. Does someone have another idea?"

The student who was a realtor commented, "In my office, the rewards given to employees are often related to the particular performance that is being recognized. For example, if an employee volunteered to work for another employee who was ill, the employee who volunteered is allowed to select a day of his or her choice to use as an additional vacation day."

"That sounds like a great way to encourage teamwork as well," remarked Dr. Kelly. "It sounds like individuals who are effective at praising are creative, taking the extra time and effort, which, in turn, has very positive results. That's all the time we have for this evening. Thank you for your ideas. Next week our topic in Leadership 101 will be 'The Importance of Serving as an Excellent Role Model to Others.' Before you leave, please take a few minutes to review the ideas related to the behaviors and actions of individuals who are effective at praising and providing recognition." As each student focused on the items on the blackboard, this is what they observed.

BEHAVIORS / ACTIONS OF THOSE WHO ARE EFFECTIVE AT PRAISING AND RECOGNIZING OTHERS

- They are truly happy for the success of others.

- They utilize a variety of techniques when praising.

- They are specific in defining the reason for the praise and recognition.

- They relate the praise to the success of the organization.

- They praise in public which leads to additional praise from others and encouragement of others to do likewise.

- They are alert and pay special attention to initiative.

- They often relate the reward to the action being praised.

- They put forth extra effort in recognizing others.

PRAISING OTHERS
by Dr. Thomas J. Shaughnessy
APRIL 9, 1998

Praising others is a great way to build their self-esteem,
And remember that the stronger the individual, the better the team.
Sincere praise also boosts the other person's productivity,
For recognition is truly appreciated for reasons ranging from A to Z.

When leaders praise their employees, they also gain their respect,
For it shows the leader's paying attention and time does not neglect.
Praising improves relationships; so much good it brings,
Helping ordinary people do extraordinary things.

Praise helps create a much more positive work atmosphere,
Enhancing everyone it touches as it impacts each one's career,
And employee turnover can also be significantly reduced,
For praise and recognition seem to give everyone a boost.

So show that you are happy for other people's success,
And tell them exactly why they bring you such happiness.
For no matter the place or the time or condition,
Nothing is appreciated more than praise and recognition.

LESSON 9
Being an Extraordinary Role Model

As Professor Kelly walked up to the podium, he commented, "It's hard for me to believe, but we are already beginning the second half of the Leadership 101 course. Thanks to your dedication and hard work, the semester is flying by, and we are all learning a great deal about what it takes to be a highly successful individual. This evening, our topic for discussion revolves around being an extraordinary role model. As always, we will begin the class by discussing some of the benefits of our topic for the evening. Who would like to begin the discussion?"

The student who was a police officer raised his hand and stated, "One of the significant advantages of your being an extraordinary role model is that others have much more respect for you if you follow the rules yourself."

"That's a great example," said the student who was also a middle manager. "I have always found that the best way to influence my employees is to provide them with a living example of what I expect from them. At our organization, for example, we are working very hard to reduce and eliminate sexual harassment from our business. For my part, I try to treat all employees, both men and women, with the respect that they deserve. I have found that by doing this, I also gain their respect in return."

"Those are excellent ideas," responded Professor Kelly. "In my management classes I have always emphasized the fact that to lead successfully, a manager must have the respect of the employees, and as has been pointed out, one of the best ways to earn the respect of others is to serve as an excellent role model. Does someone else have another example of a benefit of being an extraordinary role model?"

The student who was an entrepreneur suggested, "One of the primary benefits of serving as an extraordinary role model is that it enhances the productivity of the organization."

"Could you give us an example of this?" asked Dr. Kelly.

The entrepreneur suggested, "For example, if the owner of a small business arrives promptly to work each day, it is much more likely that the employees will arrive on time as well. The same can be said regarding other areas such as following the appropriate dress code, following organizational policies, and so forth."

Professor Kelly complimented the student for his remarks and stated, "It is said that what we do has a much greater impact on others than what we say. The examples provided by the entrepreneur support this theory quite well. Does anyone else have yet another benefit of being an extraordinary role model?"

The student who was a nurse commented, "As an employee, I think that it is so important to have a supervisor as an excellent role model. This enhances the entire work atmosphere because the employees are more comfortable having such a leader to depend on. Let's face it, the supervisor is the most influential individual when it comes to influencing the future of each employee, and it's nice being able to feel good about the person you report to."

"You have hit upon a significant benefit of being an extraordinary role model," said Professor Kelly. "We all have an impact on those around us both in our careers and in our personal lives. If a parent tells his child never to drink alcoholic beverages yet consumes them himself or herself, the child is more likely to follow the parent's behavior rather than his or her suggestion. The same is true in the world of work."

The student who was a counselor raised her hand and said, "One of the things that I have learned in my years as a counselor is that we are always making an impression, whether we want to or not. We might as well make it a good one."

"You are so right," stated Dr. Kelly. "Whether we are in a classroom such as this one, at work, or with our loved ones, we continue to make impressions on those around us. It is mind-boggling to consider the influence we have as we live our lives. Most of us are surrounded by people throughout our days and evenings. It is impossible not to be making an impression and, therefore, influencing the people we associate with. Does anyone else have an example of a benefit of being an extraordinary role model?"

The student who was also a pastor raised his hand and suggested, "While it is true that a benefit of being extraordinary role models is the positive impact we have on others, it is also beneficial as a way to boost the self-esteem of the individuals who serve as effective role models."

"How true that is," said Professor Kelly. "Nothing is more satisfying than having a positive impact on other people. For example, as supervisors of young people beginning their career, we can teach them things that will enhance their performance throughout their lives. You might say that serving as an extraordinary role model is a form of nonverbal communication in that we often communicate through our actions rather than through words. Does someone else have yet another benefit of serving as a positive role model?"

The student who was a stockbroker suggested, "I believe that a benefit of being an extraordinary role model is that it helps both the individual role model and those around him or her enjoy their careers more. When we go to work knowing that we make a positive difference in the lives of others, we gain more satisfaction and enjoy our careers more. It's a great feeling looking forward to going to work each day."

"Thank you," said Professor Kelly. "Without question, most people spend more time at work than in any other aspect of life. We might as well enjoy ourselves, and knowing that we serve as excellent role models makes a major contribution to our satisfaction and enjoyment. It's time to move on to the second half of this evening's session. First, take a look at the list of benefits you came up with that relate to serving as an extraordinary role model. As the students in the Leadership 101 class examined the items on the board, this is what they viewed.

BENEFITS OF BEING AN EXTRAORDINARY ROLE MODEL

- Others have greater respect for you.
- The productivity of the organization is enhanced.
- Those around you are more comfortable.
- The role model serves as a positive example to others.
- Serving as a role model also enhances the self-esteem of the role model.
- The role model and those around him or her enjoy their career more.

Professor Kelly began the second half of the evening's session by saying, "As you can see, being an extraordinary role model is one of the most vital keys to success because of the impact it has on enhancing the performance of the people who surround such a person. Whether in our careers or personal lives, we all want to be excellent role models. But how do we do it? What are the behaviors and actions of such people? This is our challenge for the rest of this evening's session as we describe the behaviors and actions of extraordinary role models. Who would like to get us started on this pivotal topic?"

The student who was also a factory worker began the discussion by saying, "One of the keys to being a good role model is to be well-organized. I have learned that before I begin my day, I must make sure to have all of my tools available so that there are no delays once I begin my work. New workers often come to me and ask me for suggestions. I always tell them to get organized at the beginning of the day as it sets the tone for the entire day. It seems to be something that others not only notice but also apply themselves."

"Thank you," said Dr. Kelly. "Being well-organized is certainly one of the foundations of success and is easily recognized by others. Who else has a behavior or action of people who are excellent role models?"

The student who was a medical doctor raised his hand and said, "Please don't laugh when I suggest that extraordinary role models are prompt. Doctors have a reputation of keeping their patients waiting for long periods of time, and certainly many doctors deserve this reputation. However, in my practice, we pride ourselves on promptness and typically serve our patients within ten minutes or less of their scheduled appointment time."

The students in the class applauded.

The doctor went on, "At every staff meeting, I emphasize to all of the employees the importance of time both to ourselves and especially to our patients. It is amazing how many new patients we have generated through our promptness. Something that I have learned is that it all starts with me. As the doctor, I realize that if I don't set the example by providing prompt, efficient service, my employees won't either."

"Thank you very much," said Professor Kelly. "None of us wants to waste our time, and people definitely notice and appreciate our being prompt in the performance of our jobs. Who else has an idea as to a behavior or action of an extraordinary role model?"

The student who was a human resource manager commented, "It was mentioned earlier that excellent role models are well-organized and begin each day by getting prepared for the work of the day. Also related to this is the fact that extraordinary role models live and work according to priorities. We often hear the expression 'work smart,' and working according to priorities is one of the best ways to do this."

"Excellent observations," acknowledged Professor Kelly. "Certainly by living and working according to priorities, we not only are more successful in what we do but also provide a great example to those around us as to what it takes to be successful in all aspects of life. Simply put, highly successful people live according to priorities. Does someone else have another example of a behavior or action of extraordinary role models?"

The student who was an electrician said, "One of the best ways I know to be an extraordinary role model is to care about those around me. It's too easy to get in a hurry, thinking only of myself. On many occasions, I find myself working on a project which may not seem to be of great importance to me, but it is to my customer. I always try to take the extra time to ask questions about matters that the customer would never even think of. Also, when I make suggestions that will result in an improvement, the customers are very appreciative. They also treat me with more respect. Does it pay off? Besides the satisfaction it gives me from a job well done, most of my current business is through referrals of satisfied customers."

"Thank you very much," replied Professor Kelly. "Without question, caring about others in our work and personal lives usually has positive results for everyone. Does someone have yet another example of a behavior or action of people who are great role models?"

The student who was an architect suggested, "One of the behaviors of people who are excellent role models is that they keep their promises. When I tell clients that their project will be done in ten weeks, I do whatever is necessary to complete the project as promised. My employees know this and work hard to help me complete the work in a timely matter. As the doctor stated earlier, it all begins with me. If I don't provide the information my employees need promptly, they see no need to complete their assignments on schedule. We then hope that our customers pay the bill on time."

"Thank you for your ideas," said Dr. Kelly. "Keeping promises is certainly a behavior that rubs off on those around us both in our work and personal lives. Any other ideas as to behaviors and actions of extraordinary role models?"

The student who was a business executive stated, "As I was striving to move up the organizational ladder, I took notes as to what the most successful people in the organization were like, particularly what made them unique. One of the things that I discovered is that the highly successful individuals were continuously searching for ways to improve. No matter how successful they had already been, they were always striving to enhance their abilities and their chances for a promotion."

"Thank you," said Professor Kelly. "Without question, in this rapidly changing world, continuous improvement has become a way of life for those of us seeking to be successful. What an impact this can have on those around us. It is vital that we encourage those around us to seek ways to improve. For example, I distribute a form called a self-analysis in all of my classes, hoping that by reflecting on strengths and weaknesses, priorities and interests, personal and career-related goals, my students will make discoveries that allow them to continually improve their prospects for success, happiness, and satisfaction in all aspects of their lives. Does someone have another idea to share?"

The student who was the manager of a department store suggested, "In the retail business, I feel that appearance is very important. One of the topics we discuss at many of our store meetings is the impact our appearance has on our customers. If a customer is shopping for a suit, and my employee is wearing blue jeans, the customer is not likely to view the employee as a professional, at least not when selling suits. My employees have also suggested that they feel more confident when they are dressed appropriately. In a department store, there are many departments, and what is appropriate appearance in one area may differ significantly from others. However, good grooming and cleanliness are always important."

"Thank you," agreed Dr. Kelly. "Undoubtedly, personal appearance is one of the most obvious ways we can influence others. As the department store manager stated, appropriateness for the situation is the key. Does someone else have an example of a behavior or action of an extraordinary role model?"

The student who was a taxi driver said, "I have found that being pleasant to my customers is very helpful. As a taxi driver, many of my customers are in a big hurry, even upset about being late. I try to calm them down by being considerate and pleasant. I try to compliment them in some way, smile when I greet them, and just let them know how much I appreciate the opportunity to serve their needs. While these do not always work, I find that many of them become more positive and pleasant themselves."

"Those are excellent observations," said Dr. Kelly. Being pleasant to others is one of the best ways to improve their attitude. You are all doing a great job as usual. Does someone have yet another example of a behavior or action of an excellent role model?"

The student who was a high school softball coach commented, "Something that I try to do in developing the character of the young women on my team is to admit when I make mistakes. In the excitement of a game, many times I have sent a runner home when I should have held her back. When this happens, the first thing I do is to let her know that it was my fault, not hers. As the season progresses, I have noticed many of my players similarly apologizing to other players when they make a mistake. It sure feels good to see the maturity and development of the players, knowing that my behavior had something to do with it."

"Thank you very much," said Professor Kelly. "As we can see, being an extraordinary role model can have a very positive impact on the lives of others. Does someone have another idea to share?"

The student who was a supervisor suggested, "Great role models tend to give credit to those who deserve it. It's amazing how some people not only fail to give recognition to those who deserve it but also even try to steal the credit for themselves. My employees know that they can come to me with their ideas because I will make sure that they get the credit. The funny thing is that by giving credit to those who deserve it, I also come out ahead in the long run. It seems to rub off because my employees often praise their co-workers on accomplishments that they have completed as a team."

"Thank you very much," remarked Dr. Kelly. "Praising others is a great way to influence others to do likewise. Does someone else have another behavior or action that effective role models often exhibit?"

The student who was also a husband commented, "Something that I noticed about my wife when we first met years ago was that she often went beyond what was expected. She is one of the most considerate people I have ever known and often surprises people with her thoughtfulness."

"Thank you," noted Dr. Kelly. "An important characteristic of people who are extraordinary role models is that they truly do extraordinary things, going beyond the expectations of others. The golden rule suggests that we 'do unto others as we would have them do unto us,' but exceptional role models truly go beyond these expectations, applying what I like to call the 'platinum rule.' Great role models thus teach others to do likewise. Something that I was reminded of as I listened to the gentleman describing his wife is that extraordinary role models are typically highly ethical individuals who help others not to gain recognition but simply to be of service to others. Thank you once again for doing an outstanding job in sharing 94 your ideas. Our topic for next week's class is 'The Importance of Teamwork to Our Success.' Before leaving, please take the time to review the list of excellent ideas you came up with regarding the behaviors and actions of people who are extraordinary role models." As the students reviewed the items on the board, this is what they saw.

BEHAVIORS / ACTIONS OF EXTRAORDINARY ROLE MODELS

- Extraordinary role models are well-organized.

- Extraordinary role models are prompt.

- They live according to life and career priorities.

- They truly care about the needs of others.

- They keep their promises.

- They continuously seek ways to improve further.

- They have professional / appropriate appearance.

- They are pleasant to those around them.

- They admit when they make a mistake.

- They gladly give credit to others.

- They go beyond the expectations of others.

BEING AN EXTRAORDINARY ROLE MODEL
by Dr. Thomas J. Shaughnessy
JUNE 11, 1998

Being a role model is a role we all must play,
Whether at the office or at home, each and every day.
Being an excellent role model is a way to earn respect,
And if you seek promotions, it is you they will select.

For excellence also results in high productivity for you and others,
For they enjoy working with you; it's a joy, not a bother.
While you are working well with others, working jointly as a team,
You will also feel good about yourself and have a healthy self-esteem.

It's important to be well-organized, living by priorities,
To be prompt in all your duties so your boss will be quite pleased.
Show you care for those around you and keep the promises you make,
And dress professionally and appropriately; your reputation is at stake.

Continuously strive to improve in those areas you highly value.
Be pleasant to the people in your life, and your success will astound you.
Always readily admit when you make mistakes along the way.
It's simply called being human; what more is there left to say?

Cheerfully credit others for the good deeds that they've done.
And go beyond others' expectations, and life's challenge you'll have won.
For we all make impressions on others, whether we choose to or not.
So go out there and be your best and always give it all you've got.

LESSON 10
Emphasizing Teamwork

Professor Kelly walked into the room and greeted the Leadership 101 students by saying, "I am particularly excited about this evening's session because our topic is 'Emphasizing Teamwork.' As you probably all know, teamwork has never been more important or as widely emphasized in the workplace, in publications, in seminars and in books as it is today. There are good reasons for this as we will discover together this evening. Without wasting any time, let's work together as a team as we have always done and share some of the many benefits of emphasizing team-work as we strive for success. Who would like to get us started?"

The student who was a middle manager commented, "What amazes me the most about the power of teamwork is that the productivity of my division goes up dramatically when we work together."

"Thank you," said Dr. Kelly. "What the manager is suggesting is that through teamwork, a synergy is created. Synergy suggests that the whole is greater than the sum of its parts; thus, two or more people working together as a team are more productive than the combined total of their productivity when they work as individuals. Synergy occurs both at work and in our personal lives. By working together, we are able to do things that could not be done by individuals. The power of teamwork is amazing in large part due to the brainstorming that takes place as we learn from each other and also as we use each other's ideas as spring-boards to our own. Just as this occurs each evening in the Leadership 101 class, teamwork similarly unleashes similar productivity gains in the workplace. Productivity is so important in the workplace that if it was the only benefit of teamwork, it would be enough to make it worthwhile. But as we shall see, there are many additional benefits of teamwork. Who has one of these other benefits to share?"

The student who was a human resource manager stated, "Another significant advantage of teamwork is that it strengthens the cohesiveness of the employees, both managers and nonmanagers alike. By its very nature, teamwork requires that people work together, and as they work together, they get to know each other and often begin to care about each other, to assist each other, and so on."

"Thank you very much," added Professor Kelly. "It's been stated before in the Leadership 101 class that most of us spend more time at work than in any other aspect of our lives, so it's very important that we feel good about not only the work we do but also the people we work with. Teamwork makes a major contribution to help us get to know the people we work with and to the positive human relations we all seek. It's sure nice working somewhere where the morale is high on a regular basis. Does someone else have another benefit of teamwork to describe?"

The student who was a secretary said, "One of the things I like best about teamwork is that the level of stress I feel is greatly reduced. I've worked in situations where I feel like everything is up to me, getting no help from anyone else. This atmosphere creates a lot of discomfort and stress. I'm happy to say that I am now working in an organization that emphasizes teamwork. We all see ourselves as resources who are happy to assist each other whenever possible. As the saying goes, 'There's strength in numbers.' "

"Thank you for your comments," said Dr. Kelly. "Without question, feeling like you're out there on your own can be very stressful. Effective teamwork provides peace of mind in knowing that we have others we can count on for assistance when we need it. It is important to keep in mind that the best way to surround ourselves with resources is to serve willingly as a resource to others as well. Does someone have yet another idea as to the benefits of teamwork?"

The student who worked in a factory said, "One of the things that I like best about the new emphasis on teamwork is that everyone gets to participate. In the past, employees were simply told what to do and often felt left out of the decision making entirely. Today, I'm more excited about going to work because I feel that I'm more important to the success of my organization."

"Thank you," responded Dr. Kelly. "You have hit upon one of the key benefits of teamwork, which is the utilization of all employees, not just a few. Often nonmanagement employees come up with the best ideas, sometimes because they are closer to the work and often because they deal directly with the customers. The employee in the team-focused environment of today plays a pivotal role in the success of the organization. Teamwork is thus beneficial to both the employee and the organization.

Does someone have another benefit related to teamwork to share?"

The student who was a department store manager commented, "Since we have incorporated teamwork in our business, we have noticed a reduction in employee turnover. One of the reasons as mentioned is that employees are more motivated to work in an environment in which they are asked to fully participate. Also, due to the increased involvement, more employees benefit from rewards such as bonuses because of their suggestions for improving the organization."

"Excellent idea," noted Professor Kelly. Does anyone have another idea to share?"

The student who was a computer software specialist said, "One of the benefits of teamwork is that communication is much more open. As team members, employees meet regularly both at scheduled team meetings and on an as-needed basis, depending on the project that team members are working on."

"Without question, teamwork is an effective way to enhance the communications, which are beneficial to both the employees and the organization," said Professor Kelly. "Communications are essential to the success of all organizations, so the improvement due to teamwork is one of the primary benefits of teamwork in the workplace. Does anyone have another suggestion as to the benefits of teamwork?"

The student who was a supervisor suggested, "Teamwork has made me a more effective manager. Just as teamwork is good for the employees and the organization, it is beneficial to managers in that it allows them to delegate tasks to the team members."

"Thank you very much," agreed Dr. Kelly. "It's true that teamwork provides leaders with the opportunity to work more closely with their employees, including the ability to delegate tasks to the various teams or members of teams. Any other ideas?"

The student who was a nurse said, "At my place of employment, teams seem to have helped all of us, the doctor, nurses, and other staff members, to focus on the priority objectives of the office. It is so easy to get off track when we are each doing our own thing, but the team has helped us to focus on the key goals."

"Excellent ideas," said Dr. Kelly. "Often we get so caught up in our own activities that we fail to consider if we are contributing to the achievement of the mission of the business. Teamwork encourages us to do just that: create a feeling of unity. That's a good place to wrap up our discussion on the benefits of emphasizing teamwork in the workplace. Before moving on to our discussion regarding the behaviors and actions of leaders who emphasize teamwork, take the time to ponder the outstanding list of benefits you created this evening." As the students reviewed the items on the board, this is what they observed.

BENEFITS OF EMPHASIZING TEAMWORK

- Teamwork dramatically improves productivity.

- Teamwork strengthens the cohesiveness of employees.

- Teamwork improves employee morale.

- Teamwork also reduces the amount of stress.

- Teamwork encourages / requires the use of resources.

- Through teamwork everyone gets to participate.

- Teamwork leads to a reduction in employee turnover.

- Teamwork opens up communication channels.

- Teamwork improves the effectiveness of many managers.

- Teamwork helps everyone focus on priority objectives.

Professor Kelly said, "It's time to begin the second half of this evening's session, in which we will list the behaviors and actions of leaders who emphasize teamwork. We know how important teamwork is to our success, but how does one encourage teamwork through his or her behaviors and actions? Who would like to get us started?"

The student who was an executive suggested, "Leaders who promote leadership establish a variety of teams, seeking to involve all employees on at least one team. The employee should be encouraged to select a team that he or she feels particularly passionate about. For example, if the employee is strongly committed to reducing employee turnover, then he or she should join the particular team that seeks to reduce turnover."

"Thank you," said Dr. Kelly. "It's always best to allow employees to select teams that they are enthused about. The types of teams to be created can be as unique as the needs of the organization. Does someone have another example of a behavior or action of leaders who emphasize team-work?"

The student who was an entrepreneur stated, "In my business, I try to encourage teams by rewarding the accomplishments of the teams. The rewards vary a great deal, including things like money, time off, donuts, t-shirts, dinners at local restaurants, and so on. The main thing is that employees appreciate being recognized and rewarded for their efforts."

"Thank you very much," said Professor Kelly. "No doubt about the fact that people love receiving rewards for their efforts, and rewarding team members encourages teamwork by all employees. Does someone else have an idea related to our topic?"

The student who was a salesperson said, "The best leaders provide assistance to their employees. My current supervisor helps get the team's efforts rolling by making suggestions as to particular resources we might utilize in our efforts. Since she has been with the organization longer than the rest of us, she knows a great deal about shortcuts and the right people to contact regarding various team projects."

"That's a very good idea," noted Dr. Kelly. "Effective leaders often serve as a catalyst for team members by offering suggestions, letting the team members know that they are happy to help whenever assistance is needed. Does anyone have another idea to share?"

The student who was a D.J. at a radio station said, "Where I work, the leader encourages teamwork by involving everyone at employee meet-ings. There are usually one or two individuals who are more assertive than the rest, and these individuals can unknowingly dominate meetings and team projects. Our leader compliments their efforts at each meeting but also regularly emphasizes the importance in what he calls 'consensus projects,' which are team projects that he wants every single employee to make contributions to."

"What a great idea," acknowledged Professor Kelly. "By requiring that everyone gets involved in projects, the leader is ensuring that through the input of everyone, all employees feel important in the attainment of the objectives, and typically the results are better when compared to projects dominated by a few individuals. Who else has an idea to share with the group?"

The student who was a stockbroker suggested, "In my office, the company brings in speakers who deal with special topics. Not long ago, the topic of the session was brainstorming. At this session the speaker emphasized that brainstorming is only as effective as the group of employees allows it to be. He also commented that if we all see ourselves as on the same team, the results of the brainstorming sessions will be much more satisfactory."

"Excellent idea," responded Dr. Kelly. "By discussing related topics such as brainstorming, consensus decision making and so on, the teams are bound to be more effective. Does someone else have an idea to share?"

The student who was a realtor commented, "In my workplace, much of the time we are each doing our own thing, so our office manager occasionally gives us a project that requires the combined efforts of all of us, which helps us both to appreciate the value of the other members of the organization and to encourage us to utilize others more often than we would otherwise do."

"Thank you," remarked Professor Kelly. "Too often we get wrapped up in our own little world. By utilizing others regularly, we enhance our success significantly and develop stronger relationships with others. Are there any other ideas to share on our topic for this evening?"

The student who was a secretary suggested, "In my organization we utilize teamwork regularly as a type of cross-training. This is beneficial in numerous ways. For example, during the summer months many of our employees take vacations. Through the cross-training developed through teamwork, it is easier to allow more flexibility as to scheduling vacations because other employees are able to step in and keep things running smoothly during the absence of other employees."

"Thank you for your input," said Dr. Kelly. "The cross-training aspect of teamwork has become even more important as many organizations have reduced the total number of employees, leaving fewer people to carry on the work. Any other ideas?"

The student who was a police officer said, "Where I work, we try to make sure that the teams result in 'friendly' competition. There are a lot of highly competitive individuals who can take the team concept the wrong way, thinking it's an us-against-them situation."

"Great idea," acknowledged Dr. Kelly. "The teams must be organized in such a manner that the key is to move the organization closer to its priority objectives. The teams must also be rewarded in such a manner that all feel positive about the success of every team, both those that they are a part of directly and those that they are indirectly a part of as organization members. Many times when I speak to people who truly love their place of employment, they comment as to how a type of 'family' atmosphere is created. Teams can indeed create this type of environment, one in which we all realize that we truly are 'all in this together.' We've run out of time this evening. Our topic for next week's session is 'The Importance of Being Loyal' to those around you and to your organization. Before leaving, take a few minutes to reflect on the ideas you've shared regarding the behaviors and actions of leaders who are effective in encouraging teamwork." As the students looked at the items on the board, this is what they perceived.

BEHAVIORS / ACTIONS OF LEADERS WHO EMPHASIZE TEAMWORK

- Leader establishes a wide variety of teams.

- Effective leader rewards team accomplishments.

- Leader makes suggestions as to the resources to be utilized.

- Leader encourages participation by everyone at meetings.

- Leader provides seminars / programs related to teamwork.

- Leader assigns projects requiring teamwork.

- Leader uses teamwork as a form of cross-training.

- Leader encourages "friendly" competition among the teams.

- Leader uses teams to create a "family" atmosphere.

EMPHASIZING TEAMWORK
by Dr. Thomas J. Shaughnessy
JUNE 19, 1998

Teamwork has become essential in boosting organizational performance.
As it strengthens the cohesiveness of everyone, its impact is enormous.
At the same time it enhances morale, it also reduces stress,
Encouraging the use of resources and "consensus participation," nothing less.

Teamwork encourages people to remain, thus reducing employee turnover,
Opening channels of communication, a complete organizational makeover.
It also makes leaders more effective as it requires regular delegation,
Helping all focus on priority objectives and reducing waste and frustration.

Great leaders establish many teams, each with a unique purpose,
Allowing each employee to choose the one(s) so that all can be of service.
Rewards that are distributed are as varied as the people who receive them,
But what's common is the boost in self-esteem in those who achieve them.

Effective leaders make recommendations, suggesting resources to utilize,
And involve everyone at meetings as the importance of all they realize.
So seminars are provided on topics related to the use of teams,
Assigning team projects as well, for it takes all of us to reach our dreams.

The teams help cross-train everyone, so we can better work together.
As our competition is friendly and unified, we will remain forever.
We get up for work each morning with a smile upon our face,
For our teams result in a family atmosphere and a positive workplace.

LESSON 11
Loyalty

Professor Kelly walked purposefully up to the podium and said, "We are in for another exciting session. The topic we are about to discuss is vital to the success of both individuals and organizations yet is often lacking. Our topic is 'Loyalty,' suggesting that it is important to be loyal to both the people around us and the organizations we are members of such as families, community organizations, and places of employment. It is all too common that both individuals and organizations are self-centered, thinking only of themselves. This is damaging to all concerned. Loyalty suggests that we take a broader perspective, considering the needs and wants of others as we live our lives. As I mentioned, tonight's discussion should be very exciting and beneficial to all of us. Who would like to begin the discussion revolving around the benefits of loyalty?"

The student who was a waitress said, "One of the benefits of being loyal to others is that you gain their respect. I have a supervisor who always stands up for those of us who work for her. Without a doubt it's one of the main reasons that she has the respect of everyone in the restaurant."

"Thank you," acknowledged Dr. Kelly. "Being loyal is certainly one of the best ways to gain the respect of others. Does someone have another benefit of loyalty to share?"

The student who was an accountant suggested, "By being loyal to others, you receive more ideas from them. They know they can count on you for support, so they are more than happy to share their thoughts with you."

"Good idea," responded Professor Kelly. "A major benefit of loyalty to others is that it significantly increases the amount of communication you receive. Therefore, while your loyalty toward others is beneficial to them, the ideas you receive can enhance your life and career as well. Who has another idea to share?"

The student who was a middle manager commented, "By being loyal to others, you also gain additional ideas because it broadens your perspective."

"Could you give us an example of this?" asked Dr. Kelly.

The student continued, "For example, when you only see things from your own point of view, you have a type of tunnel vision or a narrow perspective. When you consider the needs of others such as customers or co-workers you attain additional ideas. If a salesperson is loyal to his or her customers, he or she will ask questions to determine the customers' specific needs and wants. Similarly, a manager who really cares about employees will gain ideas by looking at situations from the employees' perspective."

"Thank you very much," said Dr. Kelly. "As we can all see, loyalty to others is beneficial in numerous ways. Does someone else have another benefit of loyalty to share?"

The student who was a pastor suggested, "Individuals who are loyal to others are less likely to gossip about them, for being loyal leads to being more considerate of others."

"Thank you," echoed Dr. Kelly. "It is easy to see that this would lead to an excellent reputation. As you might guess, people who are loyal to others think before speaking and follow Will Rogers' philosophy by not saying anything about someone unless they can say something nice. Does anyone have another idea to share regarding the benefits of loyalty to others?"

The student who was an executive commented, "One of the benefits of loyalty is that it significantly enhances the opportunity one has of attaining a promotion. Many factors are considered, but loyalty is a must when it comes to achieving a promotion."

"Thank you," replied Dr. Kelly. "Loyalty is a quality that impresses both supervisors and employees. It is easy to see why loyalty enhances your opportunities for receiving a promotion. Are there any other ideas regarding the benefits of loyalty?"

The student who was the manager of a department store shared, "Loyalty indicates that the individual has made a commitment to the organization. Every employer hopes to retain the services of his or her employees for a long period of time, and loyalty is a quality that says, 'I'm in this for the long haul,' which is music to the ears from a leader's point of view."

"Thank you very much," agreed Professor Kelly. "As mentioned earlier, loyalty is a scarce quality, and those who demonstrate this trait are prized by their supervisors. Does someone else have another idea to share?"

The student who operated a daycare said, "I try to be loyal to my employees, realizing that my organization's employee turnover will be reduced. It's very expensive to hire and train new employees, and I have found that one of the best ways to keep turnover low is to show loyalty to the employees we already have."

"Thank you," remarked Dr. Kelly. "When employers demonstrate loyalty to employees, the employees are much more likely to remain with the organization, which is their way of returning the loyalty that they have been shown. Well, it's time to move on to our second half of this evening's session. Before we do, take some time to consider the ideas you came up with regarding the benefits of being loyal to others and to the organization." As the students gazed at the items on the board, this is what they noted.

BENEFITS OF LOYALTY

- Loyalty helps an individual gain the respect of others.
- Loyalty helps a person gain more ideas from others.
- Loyalty broadens one's perspective.
- Loyalty reduces the likelihood of gossiping.
- Loyalty improves one's reputation.
- Loyalty enhances the likelihood of a promotion.
- Loyalty indicates that you've made a commitment.
- Loyalty can help reduce employee turnover.

"Time to move on to the second half of this evening's session," stated Professor Kelly, who was just as eager to get started as the students. "We have listed many of the benefits of loyalty, and we are now about to uncover many of the actual behaviors and actions that give one the reputation of being a person who is loyal. The loyalty we are discussing may be focused on our loved ones, customers, or business associates. Who would like to begin the discussion?"

The student who was a factory worker responded, "To me, a person who is loyal supports those around him or her. For example, the best supervisor I ever had was very supportive of employee ideas even if the idea did not agree with the current policy. The supervisor was concerned most with what was right and wrong, not whose idea it was."

"Thank you very much," said Dr. Kelly. "It's true that a good supervisor supports his or her employees. Who has another idea?"

The student who was a retiree commented, "I like the idea that the other student just shared about supporting what's right and wrong. Sometimes the supervisor supports company policy by requiring all employees to follow the policies of the organization. Most importantly, the supervisors follow the policies themselves."

"Thank you," responded Dr. Kelly. "Loyalty moves in various directions and sometimes is focused on the company we work for as we follow rules, policies, and other guidelines. Who has yet another idea to share?"

The student who was a chiropractor said, "One of the best ways to show loyalty to others is to share only positive remarks about them when speaking to others. People who are loyal to others do not spread negative gossip."

"Excellent remarks," acknowledged Professor Kelly. "If we are truly loyal to others, we do not gossip about them. This may tarnish their reputation and will definitely tarnish our reputation as the person who is known as a gossip. Who would like to share another idea with the group?"

The student who was a supervisor said, "As a supervisor, I have learned that being totally honest at all times is one of the best and simplest ways to be loyal to my employees and to my organization."

"Thank you very much," agreed Dr. Kelly. "It may sound corny, but honesty really is the best policy. People may not always agree with you, but they will respect you if you are honest in your dealings with them. Does someone else have an idea to share?"

The student who was a waitress suggested, "People who are loyal to others pitch in and help them out whenever possible. I believe this shows that they are loyal to those they are helping and to the business they work for."

"Thank you for your suggestions," approved Dr. Kelly. "Without a doubt, pitching in to help others when they need us most is one of the best ways to show our loyalty to them and to gain their loyalty in return. Could someone else add another idea to those we've already suggested?"

The student who was an electrician said, "As simple as it may sound, I believe the best way I can show loyalty to both my customers and my company is to always do my best. Most of the time, I am working by myself. Although it would be easy to slack off, this would not be good for my customer or my company. I always try to be thorough in every job I complete. In the long run, it pays off in that many of my former customers ask for me when they call about a problem."

"Thank you," affirmed Dr. Kelly. "Many of us work in situations where it would be easy to waste time during the work day. In the long run, by doing our best, we develop reputations as excellent employees who show loyalty by working efficiently. Does someone else have an idea to share?"

The student who was a middle manager said, "One of the ways I show my loyalty to my employees is to keep them informed. Most of the time, I get information before my employees do. As soon as I get information, I try to share it with those individuals who need it to do their jobs effectively."

"Thank you," agreed Dr. Kelly. "By sharing information with those who need it, we are illustrating loyalty to those individuals, the organization, and the customers who will benefit from the employees' improved performance. This is an excellent example of how loyalty and caring about others work simultaneously and improve the likelihood of our success. Does someone have yet another idea to share?"

The student who was a beautician remarked, "People who are truly loyal are happy for the success of others. In the shop where I work, one of the other beauticians is liked and respected by all of the employees. While she is successful herself, she is truly happy when the other beauticians are rewarded for their excellent performance. She often gives a congratulatory card to others and is sincerely happy for their success. She always takes the time to help the rest of us whenever she can."

"Thank you for your example," observed Dr. Kelly. "It's true that loyal people are happy for the success of those around them while those who are not loyal are often jealous or resentful. Does anyone have any other ideas to share?"

The student who was an entrepreneur said, "One of the things that I have noticed over the years is that my most loyal employees arrive promptly to work day after day. There are many people who are late most of the time, which creates problems for customers as well as other employees. Employees who are loyal arrive on time, leave only when they've completed their tasks for the day, arrive back on time after lunch breaks, and so on."

"Thank you," replied Dr. Kelly. "It seems that people who are loyal to their organization treat their work time with the same respect that they give their own time. Over the years this becomes a part of an excellent reputation, which increases the likelihood of their success. Well, our time for this evening is about up. Our topic for next week's session is 'The Quality of Being Extremely Well-organized.' Before you leave, take the time to reflect on the ideas you've shared regarding the behaviors and actions of people who are loyal." As the students reviewed the items on the board, this is what they recognized.

BEHAVIORS / ACTIONS OF PEOPLE WHO ARE LOYAL

- Loyal people support those around them.
- Loyal people support and follow company policies.
- Loyal people do not gossip about others.
- Loyal people are honest at all times.
- Loyal people pitch in and help others.
- Loyal people always do their best.
- Loyal leaders keep their employees informed.
- Loyal people are happy for the success of others.
- Loyal people are honest.

LOYALTY
by Dr. Thomas J. Shaughnessy
JULY 13, 1998

Loyalty is a quality that will benefit you in many ways.
Gaining the respect of others is but one that will help you day by day.
Those who are loyal also receive more ideas from those around them,
Sometimes giving the loyal persons ideas that will astound them.

For loyalty results in a significantly broader perspective,
Which in the long run makes the individual much more effective.
The loyal person refuses to participate in gossip about others
And treats everyone with the same respect reserved for sisters and brothers.

Loyalty is a quality highly regarded when handing out promotions,
For it strikes at the very core of both rationale and emotions.
Loyalty says, "Take note, for I've made a serious commitment."
And it helps reduce employee turnover as it expands one's limits.

Loyal people are supportive of the people with whom they work
And to their organizations as well; their tasks they never shirk.
Honesty is their trademark, and they always do their best,
Which helps them stand out and above most, if not all the rest.

Loyal leaders inform their employees, sharing information freely.
Finding joy in the success of others, they are caring and are really
Wonderful to have in your organization, bringing others happiness.
It is easy to understand how loyalty is a key to one's success.

LESSON 12
Being Well-organized

"Good evening everyone," Dr. Kelly said as he walked up to the podium. "This evening's topic is the importance of being well-organized. There are many who feel that this is one of the most important characteristics leading to a successful life and career. As usual, we will begin analyzing our topic by listing and describing the benefits reaped from its application. Who would like to get us started this evening?"

The student who was a doctor commented, "One of the key benefits of being well-organized is that it significantly increases your productivity. For example, in my practice I divide the hours of the week so that I can serve the needs of the most patients yet maintain the high quality of service that is necessary."

"Thank you very much," agreed Professor Kelly. "We are all busy people and, therefore, must organize the hours each day in order to achieve maximum productivity both in terms of quantity and quality. Each of us must determine what quantity and quality are appropriate for our positions. Who has another idea to share?"

The student who was a middle manager suggested, "As a manager, I think that organization is essential if one is to be considered for a promotion. It seems that those men and women who attain executive level positions do so in large part because they are extremely well-organized, working effectively by establishing priorities, and putting forth effort accordingly."

Professor Kelly commented, "There is no doubt that the organized individual establishes priorities and lives and works accordingly. Who else has an idea that they believe identifies a benefit of being well-organized?"

The student who was a taxi driver said, "By being well-organized, I make fewer mistakes. For example, I try to identify the areas of the city where I will do the most business. This varies a great deal according to the time of day, so I keep a log that I can review periodically to note the locations where I can be most profitable. By taking the time to review information in my log, I make fewer mistakes."

"Thank you for your thoughts," responded Dr. Kelly. "As you can see, being well-organized takes some planning and effort but in the long run is well worth the time as you can reduce the number of problems you encounter in your work. Who has another idea to share?"

The student who was a city councilman commented, "A major benefit of being well-organized is that you gain the respect of those around you. I have worked with many leaders both in the community and in organizations and have noticed that those individuals who are well-organized gain the respect of those around them, which makes the leader even more effective."

"Thank you," echoed Dr. Kelly. "Being organized is indeed a trait that will gain the admiration of those who work with you. Through your examples we have already established that being well-organized is extremely beneficial. However, there are still other benefits to be shared. Who would like to suggest one of these?"

The student who was a pastor commented, "One of the key benefits of being well-organized is that it allows you to delegate more effectively."

Dr. Kelly inquired, "Could you elaborate on this important benefit?"

The pastor continued, "By being well-organized, a leader is able to determine the upcoming tasks that need to be completed. These tasks are often quite diverse and require the services of many different individuals. Unless the tasks are identified, the leader is unable to line up the necessary resources, both people and otherwise, in advance."

"Thank you very much," remarked Professor Kelly. "As we can all see, being well-organized is essential to anyone who needs to assign tasks to others. Parents, managers, pastors, doctors, supervisors, and so forth are in a much better position to delegate effectively if they are well-organized. Let's move on to yet another benefit of being well-organized."

The student who was a waitress said, "In my line of work, organization is critical to satisfying the needs of the customers in a timely manner. As simple as it may sound, something like taking the customer's order requires that the menus be on the tables and that the waitress has an order form, a pen, and so on. One of the benefits of being well-organized in my line of work is that it reduces the stress because our customers are served quickly; mistakes are avoided, and everyone wins."

"Thank you for your suggestions," declared Dr. Kelly. "It's true that a great deal of stress is avoidable if only we take the time to be well-organized. Does someone else have an idea related to our topic?"

The student who was an executive suggested, "Being organized is pivotal in that it allows you to be both effective and efficient. In order to work effectively, you must first establish priorities. Once this is done, it is essential that efficiency is accomplished through the best use of available resources such as people, time, and money. All of this requires that the person be well-organized."

"Thank you very much," observed Dr. Kelly. "The evidence as to the importance of organization as it relates to our success continues to mount. Are there any other ideas to be shared?"

The student who was a DJ at a radio station said, "While the individual who is well-organized reaps many benefits, what's great about being organized is that many others benefit such as the employees of the organized manager, the customers of the organized salesperson, the children of the organized parent, and so on."

"Well put," affirmed Professor Kelly. "It's true that many people benefit due to the organizational abilities of effective individuals. Any other ideas to be shared?"

The student who was a human resource manager mentioned, "Earlier in the evening the student who is a taxi driver remarked that he keeps a log and reviews it in order to prevent mistakes. I have found that the most effective managers are well-organized, and they use a certain amount of time to reflect on things like progress towards objectives, problem areas, opportunities to be pursued, and so on."

"Thank you," responded Dr. Kelly. "Highly successful people are well- organized and establish a period of time each day to reflect on how they can become even more successful than they already are. I call this 'Reflective Improvement Time,' and it is often the most important time spent each day. We have time for one more idea if anyone has one to share."

The student who was a retiree suggested, "One of the most important benefits of being well-organized is that it raises the level of self-esteem the individual feels. It sure feels good seeing that you are living and working effectively, accomplishing your priority goals while you help others learn to do the same."

"Thank you very much," agreed Dr. Kelly. "Without question, being well-organized is one of the most important keys to being successful. Before moving on to the second half of this evening's session, please take the time to review the list of benefits you came up with that relate to being well-organized." As the students looked at the chalkboard, this is what they viewed.

BENEFITS OF BEING WELL-ORGANIZED

- It increases your productivity.
- It increases your chances for a promotion.
- It decreases the number of mistakes you make.
- It increases the amount of respect you receive.
- It significantly improves your ability to delegate.
- It reduces the amount of stress you feel.
- It allows you to be both effective and efficient.
- It is beneficial to those around you.
- It encourages "reflective improvement time."
- It increases your level of self-esteem.

Professor Kelly said, "It's time to discuss some of the behaviors and actions that demonstrate that an individual is well-organized. As is always the case, we can know how beneficial a particular success trait is, but if we do not apply it to our lives and careers, it is of no value. Who would like to get us started?"

The student who was a lawyer commented, "The well-organized individual makes planning a high priority."

"Thank you," acknowledged Dr. Kelly. "Earlier we discussed the importance of being effective and efficient and working according to priorities, and planning is the starting point. We must first reflect and plan before beginning our work. This both reduces mistakes and increases the likelihood of noticing opportunities. Who else has an idea to share?"

The student who was a supervisor suggested, "The organized person communicates both what is to be done and why it's important."

"That's a great idea," agreed Professor Kelly. "One of the benefits of explaining why a task is important is that it helps motivate the person who is to complete the task. It also requires us to examine the task or objective, verifying its importance. Who has yet another behavior or action often demonstrated by highly organized individuals?"

The student who was a human resource manager said, "Highly organized individuals often communicate nonverbally that they take pride in their roles as teachers and developers of others. Due to the motivation of the leader, the employee tends to be more motivated as well."

"Thank you for your remarks," said Dr. Kelly. As we can all see, there are numerous behaviors that demonstrate organizational skills. Who would like to share still another idea?"

The student who was a realtor commented, "Most of us attend meetings on a regular basis. The organized leaders always use an agenda and often send the agenda to the attendees in advance. This allows all of us to contribute more effectively."

"Thank you," responded Dr. Kelly. You might also say that the most effective leaders have an agenda that they live by on a regular basis. Could someone share another idea?"

The student who was an entrepreneur said, "One of the things that I have done for several years that helps keep me organized is to keep a journal. In my journal I reflect upon my priorities and what I have done to achieve them. It is important to record both the successes and failures that relate to these efforts."

"Thank you very much," declared Professor Kelly. "Keeping a journal is one of the best tools when trying to stay organized and is something that you can do by yourself. Does someone else have another idea to share?"

The student who was a middle manager said, "As a manager, I have found that keeping written job descriptions for each of my employees helps a great deal. This helps remind me what each employee should be doing. I find it is especially helpful if I rank employee tasks in priority order."

"Thank you for your ideas," observed Dr. Kelly. "I agree that well-organized leaders utilize job descriptions for each employee. They also use one for their own tasks. This has become even more important in the rapidly changing workplace of today. It is vital to keep up with the changes that affect your work and adjust your work accordingly. Does someone have an additional idea to share with the group?"

The student who was an executive stated, "Long ago I learned that it is vital to develop a personalized organizational success chart. What I mean by this is that I developed a chart much like a typical organization chart, but my chart lists the various people that I utilize as resources. I draw solid lines between the people I utilize on a regular basis and me and segmented lines between the individuals that I make use of occasionally and me."

"What a great idea," concurred Dr. Kelly. "We all need to utilize others as resources as we seek to be successful in our lives and careers. By developing and updating our own personalized success chart, we increase the benefits of such resources and remind ourselves of whom we should contact for various situations. Who else has an idea related to our topic?"

The student who was a chiropractor said, "Well-organized people think long term. Many times when we make decisions, there are numerous possible courses of action. The well-organized person considers the long-term impact of such decisions. An example of this would be how a salesperson may talk a customer into purchasing a product that is not appropriate. The sale may look good in the short run, but the long-term results will not be pleasant as customers spread the word about such unethical tactics."

"Thank you," said Professor Kelly. "It would be nice if the initial results of our decisions always corresponded to the long-term results, but this is often not the case. The organized individual thinks long term, which increases the likelihood of many years of success. Any other ideas?"

The student who was a farmer suggested, "As simple as it may seem, I have found that keeping my list of activities on a calendar has helped me keep track of things that need to be done and increases the efficiency of my use of time."

"Thank you, "replied Dr. Kelly. A calendar can be very helpful, especially when our tasks must follow a particular sequence. Does anyone have yet another idea to add to our excellent list of ideas already presented?"

The student who managed a department store stated, "One of the things that I have noticed about my most successful managers is that their organizational abilities tend to prevent many problems. My less successful managers seem to spend a lot of time fire fighting, that is, solving problems, while the more successful managers prevent many problems and thus spend most of their time creating opportunities."

"Thanks for your suggestions," agreed Professor Kelly. "So much time can be saved by preventing problems rather than coming up with solutions after the problem has already occurred. Who else has an idea to share?"

The student who was an accountant recommended, "The well-organized person tends to have a desk and office that are relatively neat. I know that we all know people who are very successful, yet their desk is a mess. By organized I am not saying that the area must be perfectly neat, but the individual must know exactly where everything is when he or she must find something. Time and frustration are saved when the desk or office is kept tidy."

"Thank you very much," said Dr. Kelly. "Whether we are talking about a closet at home or our desk at the office, having your things in order is bound to be beneficial. Does someone else have an idea to contribute?"

The student who was a secretary responded, "While I know we are living in a time which allows casual clothing certain days of the week or even on a regular basis, I still believe that personal appearance makes not only a first impression but also an ongoing impression as well. Organized people tend to dress nicely and keep themselves well groomed."

"I couldn't agree with you more," said Dr. Kelly. "Casual clothing has become more readily accepted in the workplace, but the outfit should still be well coordinated, clean, and neatly pressed. Many people I talk to say that a neat, crisp appearance not only makes an impression on others but also similarly affects the individual as well. People tend to be more confident when they look appropriate for the situation. Are there any other ideas to be shared?"

The student who was an electrician said, "The most organized people I have known always seem to have a contingency plan in case things don't go as planned."

"That's an excellent idea," agreed Professor Kelly. "In this fast-paced world, consumer preferences, product improvements, and other factors often cause us to adjust our plans in midstream. A contingency plan helps make this transition easier for all involved. One example of this is how ever-changing modern technology provides new methods of completing tasks that were nonexistent prior to these individual inventions. Well, that's all we have time for this evening. Our topic for next week's session is 'The Utilization of Resources in our Lives and Careers.' Before leaving, take a look at the ideas you shared this evening as to the behaviors and actions often exhibited by highly organized, successful individuals." As the students looked at the blackboard, this is what they observed.

BEHAVIORS / ACTIONS OF WELL-ORGANIZED LEADERS

- Leader gives planning a high priority.
- Leader communicates what is to be done and why.
- He or she takes pride in being teacher / developer of others.
- Leader prepares / distributes an agenda for all meetings.
- Leader keeps a journal to analyze successes and failures.
- He or she utilizes written job descriptions for others / self.
- Leader uses a personalized organizational success chart.
- Leader looks at the big picture . . . thinks long term.
- Leader keeps calendar listing current / upcoming projects.
- He or she prevents problems, thus spends more time on improvement.
- Leader maintains a neat office environment.
- Leader maintains a neat / suitable personal appearance.
- He or she utilizes contingency plans as needed.

THE IMPORTANCE OF BEING WELL-ORGANIZED

by Dr. Thomas J. Shaughnessy
JULY 25, 1998

Being organized contributes mightily to the success that one enjoys,
Increasing the chances for a promotion if organization one employs.
For reduced will be the mistakes while your respect will be increased.
As organization enhances the ability to delegate, much stress will be released.

The organized individual is both effective and efficient,
Benefitting those around you as each person becomes more self-sufficient.
As you record things in your journal, daily spending time reflecting
Your self-esteem will soar upward as success you're resurrecting.

Planning becomes priority one as it establishes a blueprint
And as you communicate the what's and why's to show others how to do it.
Take pride as you consider being a teacher, a developer of others,
Using agendas for formal meetings as it's worth the time and bother.

Keeping written job descriptions both for others and yourself,
Never letting them just sit there gathering dust upon some shelf.
Maintaining a personalized success chart and updating it regularly,
You are organized, plain and simple, and it's easy for anyone to see.

As you think long term in what you do, considering the big picture,
Keep a calendar of work & play, always maintaining the right mixture.
Prevention of problems is a goal, devoting time instead to improvement.
Organization provides rewards as in chess, considering each movement.

A neat desk is a common signal that people know what they're doing—
Also the appropriate personal appearance if their traits you are reviewing.
Changes often dictate a new direction, so the ability to adapt is now a must.
Utilizing contingency plans, the organized person simply adjusts.

LESSON 13
Utilizing Resources

Professor Kelly was especially excited as he walked into the Leadership 101 classroom. He knew that this evening's topic was one of the most important of all those discussed in the Leadership 101 class. Without wasting any time, he stepped up to the podium and said, "I can tell that you are all as eager to get started this evening as I am. Utilizing resources is one of the most vital keys to success both in our careers and in our personal lives as well. As always, we will spend the first half of this evening's session discussing many of the benefits of our topic. Who would like to get the ball rolling?"

The student who was a chiropractor raised his hand and said, "One of the most important benefits of utilizing resources is that productivity is increased dramatically. For example, in my practice I have a receptionist who schedules appointments and greets patients, a runner who brings the patient to the adjustment room, a patient coordinator who gathers information regarding the patient's current condition, and a physical therapist who provides therapy treatments as necessary. By utilizing these and many other resources, I'm able to spend my time providing adjustments and am able to care for many more patients."

"Thank you very much," concurred Dr. Kelly. "You have provided us with excellent examples of how utilizing resources can indeed make us more productive. Each of us must continue to reflect on how we can use our time most effectively and efficiently, and the utilization of resources is pivotal in doing just that. Who has yet another benefit of utilizing resources?"

The student who was a middle manager suggested, "I believe one of the most meaningful benefits of utilizing resources is that it leads to much more participation by those individuals utilized as resources. For example, there are always new problems and opportunities that need to be dealt with. As an individual, I cannot possibly keep up with all of them. Even if I could do it all myself, the morale of my employees would be very low if all they got to do was take orders from me. By utilizing the employees as resources, I save a great deal of time to work on other important matters while the employees feel like more important members of the organizational team."

"Thank you," agreed Professor Kelly. "As mentioned, there is nothing worse than boredom. In fact, boredom can be just as stressful and depressing as work overload. We should always keep in mind, however, that others are busy too and we should first determine their availability before utilizing them as a resource. Who else has a benefit of utilizing resources to share with the group?"

The student who was the manager of a department store commented, "By utilizing resources, the employee is illustrating his or her potential as a supervisor. All leaders depend heavily on others for accomplishing organizational goals. By utilizing others, the employee demonstrates characteristics such as initiative, motivation, people skills, and organizational skills. Thus, the employee is much more likely to be considered for a promotion than those who fail to utilize resources."

"Thank you very much," said Dr. Kelly. "In order to attain a leadership position, it is essential to demonstrate that one has the characteristics essential to succeed in such a position. Certainly, the utilization of resources is one such characteristic. Who else has an idea to share?"

The student who was a coach of a high school softball team shared, "Another benefit of utilizing resources is the continuous improvement that it brings about. Each season, as we prepare for our games, I invite an individual who puts on a clinic for a particular skill related to softball. For example, last year an individual who specializes in various bunting techniques spent a day with my team. It's exciting to see the positive results throughout the season. Each resource utilized makes us better both as individuals and as a team."

"Thank you so much for your remarks," stated Professor Kelly. "Similarly, in the business world, organizations are constantly on the lookout for ways to improve the abilities of their individuals, teams, and the organization as a whole. In fact, how many of you signed up for the Leadership 101 class because someone suggested that it would help you as you strive to be successful?" Many hands were raised. "As you can see, many of us are looking for ways to continually improve our abilities. As we move through the semester, each week all of us serve as resources to each other as we share ideas. Who has yet another idea to share regarding our topic for this evening?"

The student who was a human resource manager suggested, "One of the primary benefits of utilizing resources from an organizational point of view is that it raises the self-esteem of those individuals utilized. As we discussed earlier, most employees want to participate actively. It simply makes people feel better about themselves when they are involved as a resource to others."

"Thanks a lot," agreed Dr. Kelly. "Without question, we feel better about ourselves if others seek us out as a resource when they need help. It is one of the best forms of flattery we can receive. Does someone else have an example of how utilizing resources is beneficial to our success?"

The student who was a librarian said, "Earlier in the Leadership 101 course, the word synergy came up. I believe that by utilizing others as resources, we are creating a synergy as we work together on a task and thus accomplish more than we can as individuals."

"That is an excellent observation," declared Dr. Kelly. "Synergy is indeed created when we utilize others as resources. Brainstorming usually occurs naturally as a result of resource utilization as the individuals involved have a positive impact on each other. As you can see, the list goes on and on as to the benefits gained through the utilization of resources. Who has still another example of such a benefit?"

The student who was a pastor suggested, "Something was brought to my attention as I listened to the previous comments. A natural result of the utilization of resources is that the relationships of those individuals involved are often strengthened. Utilizing resources is nothing more than working with others rather than alone. Relationships are bound to be made as we work together on various tasks."

"Thank you for your ideas," stated Dr. Kelly. "As mentioned, a prerequisite of utilizing resources is working together, which, in turn, requires communication between the parties involved. As we work together, a bond often develops between the individuals involved, creating a closer, stronger team of individuals at the same time. Are there any other benefits to share with the group?"

The individual who was a full-time college student commented, "An advantage of utilizing resources is that the work itself becomes more interesting. In some of my classes, group projects are assigned. I have discovered that by working with others and seeking information from various resources such as other students, library materials, and local business people, the assignment is much more interesting than when I study on my own."

Thank you," said Professor Kelly. "Because each individual is unique in many ways, working with others is likely to be much more interesting than working alone. We have time for one more idea. Who would like to share another benefit of utilizing resources?"

The student who was a business executive noted, "As one continually seeks out resources, an ever-growing network is developed. This means that over time the individual becomes more effective due to the increasing number of resources at one's disposal. I also would recommend that as you develop your network of resources, seek a diversity of talents in those selected."

"Excellent ideas," acknowledged Dr. Kelly. "It's certainly true that the more diverse your resource network, the more valuable it will be to you as you strive to be successful both at work and in your personal life. It's time to move on to the second half of this evening's session. Before we do, take a few minutes to review the excellent list of benefits you shared regarding the utilization of resources." As the students reviewed the items on the blackboard, this is what they studied.

BENEFITS OF UTILIZING RESOURCES

- Productivity is increased dramatically.
- Participation by others is increased.
- The individual is more likely to be promoted.
- Continuous improvement is likely to occur.
- The self-esteem of those involved increases.
- Synergy among the participants is created.
- The relationships among the people are strengthened.
- The tasks become much more interesting.
- An ever-growing network of resources is created.

Professor Kelly began the second half of the evening's session by saying, "We all realize how important utilizing resources is to our success. We are now ready to list the behaviors and actions of individuals who utilize resources as they seek success in their careers and personal lives.

Who would like to get things started?"

The student who was an architect began, "One of the best ways to demonstrate your desire to utilize resources is to develop and utilize teams when completing tasks."

"Excellent idea," agreed Dr. Kelly. "Working in teams has become a key ingredient in the success stories of many organizations and is a great way to utilize resources. Who else has an idea to share?"

The student who was an executive stated, "I have supervised many managers at all levels of the organization, and something that I have noticed about those who effectively utilize resources is that they tend to face less stress than their counterparts who do not utilize resources."

"That makes a lot of sense," replied Dr. Kelly. "By utilizing others as we complete our assignments, much of the workload is delegated, freeing up time to reflect on vital tasks such as long-term planning, which, in turn, prevents mistakes and reduces the stress we face. Does someone else have an example of a behavior or action of individuals who effectively utilize resources?"

The student who was a computer software specialist suggested, "I have been a member of numerous teams. The best leaders not only utilize resources but also tend to utilize all team members. Some leaders only involve a few team members, creating problems among the team members who feel the leader is playing favorites."

"Thank you for your comments," said Dr. Kelly. "The best leaders try to get everyone involved, which does lead to improved relations among team members as well as improved results when the task is completed. Who could share yet another idea related to our topic?"

The student who was a human resource manager said, "Something else that the most effective leaders tend to do is to make sure that when they utilize their employees as resources, they also use it as a developmental activity. The development of one's employees is one of the most important responsibilities of those in supervisory positions. When leaders utilize resources appropriately, the organization, the leader, and the employees benefit as the employees become more valuable through the developmental activities."

"You have hit upon an excellent example of how effective the utilization of resources can be when done effectively," affirmed Dr. Kelly. "As stated, everyone benefits through the effective utilization of resources. Who else has an idea to share?"

The student who was an entrepreneur joined in by suggesting, "Something that I have noticed about the most effective leaders is that they read a lot. Most of our emphasis on utilizing resources has suggested direct contact with other people who serve as resources. There are millions of resources available in the form of books written on every topic imaginable."

"Great idea," concurred Professor Kelly. "As you have suggested, a multitude of reading materials are available if we would only take advantage of them. Many of us have probably picked up excellent ideas out of a magazine we read while waiting at a doctor's office. Bookstores and libraries are loaded with excellent materials related to your success."

A student raised her hand and said, "Professor Kelly, I believe I am speaking for all of the students when I say that the Leadership 101 class is the most practical, beneficial class I have ever taken. Have you ever thought about putting the same ideas in a book?"

"Maybe someday," responded Dr. Kelly, trying to conceal a smile. For now, who has yet another idea related to our topic of discussion?"

The student who was a wife and mother commented, "Something that highly successful people tend to do is surround themselves with excellence. This might include the people they associate with, the activities they involve themselves in, or even the physical environment of their home or office."

"Thank you very much," pondered Professor Kelly. "As our topic suggests, we should not try to complete all of our tasks on our own. If we are going to utilize others, we might as well be selective, if possible, when deciding on whom we include in our list of resources. Who has another idea related to the topic of utilizing resources?"

The student who was a first-level supervisor brought up the point, "Leaders who are most effective at utilizing resources often illustrate this by being excellent listeners. It's hard to imagine an individual who claims to want to utilize others as resources yet refuses to listen to others."

"Thank you for your suggestions," said Dr. Kelly. "It's true that if we are to be effective at utilizing others as resources, we must listen carefully to what they have to say, implementing their ideas whenever possible.

Who else has an idea to share with the group?"

The student who was a stockbroker commented, "Earlier in the Leadership 101 class, we discussed the concept of being "action-minded," that is, actively seeking out others in an attempt to gather ideas. That certainly seems appropriate as we are discussing the behaviors and actions of one who effectively utilizes resources."

"You are absolutely correct," responded Professor Kelly. "It is vital that we be action-minded as we strive to demonstrate our desire to utilize others as resources. What better way than to seek them out and ask them for their ideas? Does someone have another idea to share?"

The student who was a doctor shared, "Something that I have been trying to do as a method of utilizing my staff more effectively as resources is to conduct regular meetings. We do not have a large staff, and so we are not divided into teams. But the meetings provide another alternative as a way of gathering ideas from all staff members."

"Thank you for your idea," said Dr. Kelly. "Meetings are an excellent way to emphasize your interest in utilizing resources. It's important to be well-prepared for the meetings. Essential considerations are to send agendas in advance to those attending so that they may be ready. It is also vital to allow an adequate amount of time at each meeting for comments and responses from all attendees. Does someone else have an idea to share?"

The student who operates a daycare suggested, "It is vital to compliment anyone who shares an idea that will be beneficial to the organization, its members, or its customers. A sincere compliment is a way of indicating that you really appreciate the idea. If possible, provide rewards to those who make a positive difference through their recommendations."

"Thank you very much," commented Professor Kelly. "One of the easiest and most important ways to demonstrate the importance of resources is to praise those who serve as resources. Does anyone have yet another idea to share?"

The student who was a beautician said, "The best supervisor who I ever worked for kept us up-to-date as to the trends in the industry, her long-and short- term goals for the business, and so on. It is easier to make contributions if you know what's going on."

"Thank you," said Dr. Kelly. "The people who are most effective at utilizing others as resources share important information with them so that they can contribute to the success of the organization. Information is indeed a source of great power and must be provided to others if they are to achieve maximum productivity. Does someone have another example related to our topic of discussion?"

The student who was a retiree commented, "One of the best ways to demonstrate interest in utilizing resources is to provide the latest technology for both staff members and yourself. Imagine running a business today without any computer-related technology. Your employees would be at a tremendous disadvantage."

"Thank you," agreed Dr. Kelly. "In today's business world, technology is one of the most important resources of all in just about any type of business. How many appliances do we utilize, both at home and at work, as we complete a typical day? Are there any other ideas to share?"

The manager of a department store said, "While it is essential to gather ideas from our employees, it is just as vital to gather ideas from our customers. Let's face it, without customers, there is no business."

"Excellent observation," noted Professor Kelly. As suggested earlier, there are millions of potential resources to utilize. For almost all businesses, customers are one of the most important of these resources, and it is essential that we find ways to reach this vital resource group. Does someone have another suggestion to make?"

The student who was a factory worker commented, "One of the things I notice about effective leaders is that they treat everyone with respect. I am much more likely to volunteer ideas to help the company if I am treated as an important member of the organization."

"Thank you very much," responded Dr. Kelly. "Without question, treating others with respect is a trademark of those who are effective at utilizing others as resources. Employees will bend over backwards for such a leader. Along that same line, effective leaders tend to get to know their employees as individuals, not just as workers. By getting to know about the interests, strengths, and likes of your employees, you have a much greater opportunity to fully utilize them as resources. Does anyone have another idea to share?"

The student who was a middle manager suggested, "Those who are effective at utilizing others as resources encourage risk taking. I let my employees know up front that mistakes are considered steppingstones to success. It's easy to praise employees when everything goes well. The challenge is to compliment their efforts when the results are not what I had hoped for."

"That's a great idea," said Dr. Kelly. "Well, as is always the case, we have run out of time too quickly. Thank you for doing such a great job this evening. Our topic for next week's class is 'The Importance of Taking Time to Reflect Regularly,' such as keeping a journal. Before you leave, take a few minutes to review the ideas you came up with regarding the behaviors and actions of people who effectively utilize resources." As the students reviewed the items on the board, this is what they saw.

BEHAVIORS / ACTIONS OF THOSE WHO UTILIZE RESOURCES

- They develop and utilize teams.
- They are less stressed than others.
- They utilize all staff, not just a few favorites.
- They utilize resources as a developmental activity.
- They tend to read a lot.
- They surround themselves with excellence.
- They are excellent listeners.
- They are "action-minded."
- They conduct well-organized, regular meetings.
- They compliment the suggestions of others.
- They share information with others.
- They utilize the latest technology.
- They gather ideas from customers.
- They treat others with respect.
- They encourage risk taking.

UTILIZING RESOURCES

by Dr. Thomas J. Shaughnessy
AUGUST 11, 1998

By utilizing resources, you'll see significant gains in productivity.
You will find everyone participating, as it is clear to see,
That your promotability will be assured, as you take the very first steps,
Of continuous improvement with the help of others, as you might guess.

As you watch the self-esteem of others rise, the same may be said for you.
A synergy develops between you all, forming a bond stronger than any glue.
Relationships will be strengthened, and the work becomes more interesting.
Networks grow stronger, & you realize that resources are truly the best thing.

Successful people work in teams and reduce their stress as well,
For they utilize everyone, not just a few; they like everyone, you can tell.
As resources are used in a developmental way so that everyone benefits,
Avid readers, they surround themselves with excellence, as all the pieces fit.

They listen well to the ideas of others and, in fact, are action-minded.
Meeting with others to share information is where you'll often find them,
Complimenting the successes of others and utilizing technology
As they seek information from customers as well to create opportunities.

Treating everyone with respect is a trademark, creating a relaxed atmosphere.
They encourage risk taking by eliminating worry, concern, and fear.
The utilization of resources is extremely important, as anyone might guess.
It's difficult to imagine anything more pivotal to an individual's success.

LESSON 14
Reflective Improvement Time

Professor Kelly walked up to the podium and announced to the class, "Well, we only have two sessions left of the Leadership 101 class. You've all done a wonderful job so far in sharing ideas related to some of the most important factors in attaining success. Let's make the last two weeks the best of all. Tonight, our subjective is reflective improvement time, which is time spent in quiet reflection regarding our lives, focusing particularly on priorities whether they are related to our careers or to our personal lives. Let's begin by discussing some of the benefits of taking time to reflect on high-priority items. Who would like to begin?"

The student who was a coach commented, "Reflective improvement time is particularly important to anyone in a leadership position. As a leader, you have a responsibility to make sure that your efforts and the efforts of your group are directed toward high-priority goals. We've probably all seen college basketball coaches on television who quietly reflect for a few moments with their assistants while the players sit on the bench. This time is spent discussing strategy in a relatively calm fashion before making the final decisions as to what the players should do when they return to the floor."

"Thank you very much," stated Professor Kelly. "You are correct in suggesting that we take time for quiet reflection regularly, especially regarding strategies for achieving high-priority goals. Who else has an example of a benefit of reflective improvement time?"

The student who was a radio DJ said, "I believe that employees have more respect for leaders who take the time to think things through, which is how I view reflective improvement time."

"How true," added Dr. Kelly. "Reflective improvement time is all about thinking. Successful people typically think about an issue before making a decision, next make the decision, and finally think again about the results of the decision, which may lead to more reflection if a different strategy is necessary. Even when things are going well, it is vital to evaluate present results, trends, and so forth. Most successful people thus spend a large amount of time in reflective thinking. Who has another idea to share with the group?"

The student who was a realtor said, "Reflective improvement time is the best learning tool I have ever used. By keeping a journal, I have a permanent record of my experiences, both successes and failures."

"Thank you," agreed Dr. Kelly. "You make an excellent point in that whether we succeed or fail, we can learn from the experience. If we fail, we can analyze to determine the cause of the failure, considering alternative strategies for the future. If we succeed, we can similarly analyze to determine the specific reasons for our success. Most people simply remember that they succeeded or failed. The key is to reflect on the reasons why we succeeded or failed and apply this information to future situations. As mentioned, reflective improvement time with the use of a journal is a tremendous learning tool. Does someone else have another benefit to share?"

The student who was a middle manager said, "I find that reflective improvement time is very helpful when I am evaluating employees or myself. If I don't make the time to do this, I tend to forget many important details. By keeping a journal, I have an excellent rough draft of my employees' performance. It amazes my employees that I 'remember' so much about their performance over the past several months. A reflective improvement journal is a must for anyone in a supervisory position. An additional benefit is that the journal allows you to notice trends over an extended period of time."

"Thank you very much," said Dr. Kelly. "It's true that none of us can remember the details about the performance of others or ourselves unless we record them in a journal. Who has yet another idea to share?"

The student who was an electrician commented, "Reflective improvement time forces me to review my priorities. It is very important that I work effectively, so I must complete the highest priority tasks each day. For example, if one of my customers has a problem that could be dangerous, I try to complete that job first."

"Excellent idea," affirmed Professor Kelly. "We all must establish and live according to priorities if we are to achieve maximum success. Reflective improvement time encourages us to do just that. Does someone have another idea?"

The student who was a human resource manager mentioned, "Last week in our discussion, the subject of employee development was discussed. I believe that by keeping a journal, supervisors could use the information they gather and reflect on as a catalyst to creating a development program for each of their employees, for their entire team, and for themselves."

"Thank you very much," remarked Dr. Kelly. "As we've discussed previously, a primary responsibility of any leader is the development of his or her people. The reflective improvement journal could serve as the foundation of development programs for both individuals and teams. We have time for one more idea if anyone has one."

The student who was a pastor commented, "It seems that the bottom line regarding reflective improvement time is that it results in continuous improvement for whoever applies it."

"Thank you," echoed Professor Kelly. "One of the most common characteristics of highly successful people is that they continually improve their performance at work, in their personal lives, or both. As we have seen, regular reflective improvement time, especially with the help of a journal, can be an instrumental tool in our quest to be successful. It's time to move on to the second half of this evening's class. Before we do, take a few minutes to review the list of benefits you discussed that relate to reflective improvement time." As the students reviewed the items on the board, this is what they saw.

BENEFITS OF REFLECTIVE IMPROVEMENT TIME

- Reflective improvement time helps keep us focused on high-priority goals.
- It helps leaders gain the respect of their employees.
- Reflective improvement time is a great learning tool.
- It enhances the evaluation of others / self.
- It forces us to review priority areas.
- Reflective improvement time can serve as a base for development programs.
- Reflection leads to continuous improvement.

It was now time to begin the second half of the evening's session. Professor Kelly said, "We will now list the behaviors and actions which illustrate that an individual utilizes reflective improvement time. There are many behaviors and actions that may be observed in such an individual. Who would like to get us started?"

The student who was a city councilman stated, "People who use reflective improvement time often seek out others to gather ideas, realizing that this will significantly improve their success."

"Thank you," agreed Dr. Kelly. "By asking other people for opinions, they can see that you are serious about gathering ideas in order to improve your career and life priorities. Who has another idea to share?"

The student who was a counselor commented, "The most fundamental activity in reflective improvement is the keeping of a journal. Dr. Kelly, could you explain exactly what should be recorded in the journal?"

"I'd be happy to share a few ideas although journalizing can be as unique as the individual keeping the journal. Some items that should be recorded include the following. First of all, and perhaps most obvious, a brief description of what actually occurred should be recorded. While this should be brief, when the individual reviews the journal entries in the future, he or she should understand exactly what happened on each occasion recorded in the journal. Next, a brief description of the impact of the event should be recorded. For example, if the experience was very positive, record the specific benefits that resulted from the experience. If the experience was negative, the specific problems created should be recorded. The next step is perhaps most critical of all. Here the individual reflects and analyzes the experience to determine the specific causes of the success or failure. For example, if an individual interviews for several positions and is turned down each time, it is crucial to determine the reason or reasons. If each interviewer says that the reason is a lack of a college degree, at least the person now knows that by attaining a degree, he or she will improve the likelihood of being hired in the future. The point is whether the experience has been a success or a failure; it is vital to determine why. These are the basics of keeping a journal although each person can individualize his or her use of a journal. For example, some people have several high-priority goals to which they apply a number. If priority number one is attaining a promotion, each time they record an entry in their journal that relates to this, they put a large '1' next to the entry so that it may be easily identified as they review their journal. Other individuals use a summary page, on which they review a week or a month of entries and then summarize the most significant occurrences throughout this time period. As you can see, keeping a journal can be extremely beneficial, especially since so few people keep a journal. Therefore, it can give you a significant advantage over others. Does someone else have an idea to share with the group?"

The student who was a waitress said, "The person who uses reflective improvement time lives according to priorities."

"Thank you," said Dr. Kelly. "So many people list priorities and know what they are supposed to do but fail to do so because they get so busy doing things; as a result, they fail to take the time to think about how they are using their time. Regular reflective improvement time allows the individual to remain focused on high-priority goals on an ongoing basis. Who else has an idea to share?"

The student who was a lawyer suggested, "People who utilize reflective improvement time regularly establish a specific time each day to use for reflection."

"Thank you," commented Professor Kelly. "Individuals need to establish a specific time each day that works for them. For example, some people are early risers and might record items in their journal at 5:00 a.m., noting priorities that they will work on that day. Other individuals may conduct their reflective improvement sessions at 11:00 p.m. or even later. The time of day doesn't matter. What does matter is that you do this on a regular basis. Like any habit, getting started is the most difficult part. However, once you reap the successes resulting from your reflective improvement sessions, you will become motivated, and these sessions will become the most important part of your day and a significant part of your lifestyle. Who might have another idea?"

The student who was an executive commented, "Last week we discussed the importance of resources to our success. In keeping my journal, I give particular emphasis to determining what resources are most instrumental in helping me accomplish my goals. This allows me to fine-tune my list of resources and also reminds me to send a thank-you to the many deserving people who have helped me over the years."

"Thank you," echoed Dr. Kelly. "Too many times we fail to thank or even notice those people who make such a positive difference in our lives. The journal can help us appreciate and recognize such individuals. Does someone have another idea to add to the list?"

The student who was a nurse said, "People who reflect regularly tend to have much lower levels of stress than the majority of the population. I believe this is largely due to the fact that they notice problems in the early stages and are able to prevent them from becoming more serious."

"Thank you," replied Professor Kelly. "Just like seeing a doctor, dentist, or chiropractor regularly can help prevent serious health problems, our journals can help us prevent serious life and career problems, while also helping us take advantage of opportunities that may otherwise go unrecognized. We have time for one more suggestion. Does someone have another idea to share?"

The student who was a first-level supervisor said, "People who have learned the power of reflective improvement time and journalizing often teach others to do the same. I learned how to keep a journal a few years ago when my manager showed me how he kept his journal."

"Thank you," affirmed Dr. Kelly. "The Leadership 101 course is all about helping others become successful. Highly successful individuals often share their secrets with others and, consequently, broaden their impact. As they say, 'If you hand someone a fish, you've provided them with one meal. But if you teach them how to fish, you've provided them with food for a lifetime.' Let's hope that all Leadership 101 students share the secrets of success with others just as we share them each week in the classroom. Next week will be our final week of the Leadership 101 class. Our topic will be 'The Importance of Being Professional in our Lives and Careers.' Before leaving, take a few moments to review the list of ideas you shared regarding the behaviors and actions of an individual who incorporates reflective improvement time into his or her lifestyle." As the students reviewed the items on the blackboard, this is what they scanned.

BEHAVIORS / ACTIONS OF PEOPLE WHO USE
REFLECTIVE IMPROVEMENT TIME REGULARLY

- They seek others out for ideas.

- They keep a journal and record:
  - Describe what occurred
  - Describe the impact (positive or negative)
  - Analyze the causes of the success or failure
  - Emphasize especially high-priority goals
  - Complete summary pages weekly / monthly

- They actually "live" according to priorities.

- They establish a specific time for reflective improvement.

- They determine what resources are most helpful.

- They reduce their level of stress.

- They pass it on . . . teach others to reflect / journalize.

THE MOST IMPORTANT PART OF YOUR DAY

by Dr. Thomas J. Shaughnessy
AUGUST 14, 1998

Reflective improvement time will keep you focused on your goals,
While helping you attain the respect of others as your life unfolds.
Perhaps the greatest learning tool of all is provided by reflection
As it forces you to review priorities, steering you in the right direction.

Reflection also helps us analyze ourselves as well as evaluate others,
Creating the base for development programs one after another,
Thus leading to continuous improvement as the benefits never end.
Without question, reflective improvement time is indeed a friend.

Such people seek out others, knowing how good this can be,
As each person makes a contribution to one's success, you see.
In your journal explain what and when and why, leaving out no details,
For the ideas will provide a lift as the mountain of success you scale.

Establish a specific time of day; set aside for your reflection
And consider whom you've depended on and give them recognition.
Your life will become a joy, low in stress, so smooth and well-arranged.
Reap the benefits of your reflective time and teach others to do the same.

LESSON 15
The Professional

As Professor Kelly walked into the classroom, he noted that the students were unusually quiet. He himself was more restrained than usual. It was what he called the "last-class syndrome," as this was the final session of another Leadership 101 course. "Good evening, everyone. I can tell that you are aware that this is our final Leadership 101 class and will miss these weekly sessions. Let's make tonight's session our best ever. Our topic revolves around how being professional relates to our success. We will begin by listing many of the benefits of being professional. Who would like to get us started?"

The student who was a chiropractor said, "Being professional significantly increases the respect you receive from others, both staff members you work with as well as customers."

"Thank you very much," affirmed Dr. Kelly. "There's no doubt that a significant advantage of being professional in your work and life in general allows you to gain the respect of others, which, in turn, provides you with a much greater opportunity to positively impact their lives. For one thing, others are more likely to listen to a professional. This can certainly be critical in any relationship, whether we are referring to a career situation or an aspect of our personal lives. Who else has an idea to share?"

The student who was a stockbroker commented, "As a professional, you have more confidence in what you are doing. The preparation that is necessary to be a professional allows you to go about your work in a more positive, confident manner."

"Thank you," acknowledged Professor Kelly. "We all understand the importance of confidence in our lives and careers. Among other things, confident individuals are more proactive, taking on assignments that other individuals who lack such confidence would shy away from, missing out on significant opportunities to attain goals. Professionals are well prepared and thus are confident as they go about their lives. Does someone else have a benefit of being a professional to share with the group?"

The student who was a human resource manager suggested, "The most successful employees, in both management and nonmanagement positions, continuously seek ways to improve. Professionals tend to seek out ways to better themselves whereas many others do not."

"That's a great thought," agreed Dr. Kelly. "In this ever-changing world of ours, it is essential that we continue to seek out ideas that enhance our abilities. Because professionals do this, they remain at the top of their career area. Who has another idea related to the benefits of being a professional?"

The student who was a police officer remarked, "One of the benefits of being professional in your career is that you are able to remain objective even in emotional settings. When I am assisting people who have been in a serious accident, it is vital that I remain calm so that I can provide assistance to those injured."

"What a great example you have shared," noted Professor Kelly. "Though most of us don't usually get involved in life-and-death situations, we all must deal with emotional issues. It is essential that we remain calm and handle such situations in a calm, objective, professional manner. If we do so, we will make much better decisions. Who else has an idea to share?"

The student who was an accountant commented, "A benefit of being a professional is that you project a positive image through your personal appearance. Many times we rely heavily on our professional appearance to make a positive first impression on our clients."

"Thank you," concurred Dr. Kelly. "While the specific type of appearance that is considered appropriate varies significantly among the various career areas, the benefits we reap from looking professional, that is, appropriate for our position, are significant. Who has yet another idea to share with the group?"

The student who was a factory worker remarked, "As a professional, you have productivity that tends to be high. A professional puts in a good day's work each and every day and is usually one of the most productive employees."

"Thank you," replied Dr. Kelly. "One of the most important benefits of being professional is that you are highly productive in your work. We all know how beneficial this is to both the individual and the organization. The professional does what it takes to get the job done on a regular basis. Who else has an idea to share?"

The student who was a high school coach said, "I believe one of the most significant benefits of professionals is that they become a role model for those around them. I always try to arrive at practices before any of my players. It lets them know that I am willing to work hard to help them achieve our goals."

"Thank you very much," agreed Professor Kelly. "There are many people who influence others because of the professional status that they have achieved. It is refreshing to read about athletes, such as Mark McGwire and Sammy Sosa, because they seem to be genuinely nice people who help those less fortunate than themselves. To a certain extent, we are all role models to those around us, whether we know it or not. Professionals tend to have a positive impact on those they associate with. Does anyone else have an idea to share?"

The student who was a nurse commented, "I believe that an important benefit of being a professional is that professionals tend to perform best in the most crucial situations. It still amazes me when I observe a surgeon as he or she works feverishly to save a patient's life."

"Thank you," remarked Dr. Kelly. "The professional seems to shine brightest in the most important situations. One of the best examples of this is Michael Jordan, a professional basketball player who wants the ball in critical situations. It seems that because professionals are well prepared, they believe in themselves enough to seek out the tough assignments, which, in turn, gives them even more visibility in their organizations and professions. We have time for one more idea regarding the benefits of being a professional. Does someone have an idea to share?"

The student who was a middle manager remarked, "Because professionals are productive, one of the benefits they receive is excellent job security. In fact, in many cases other organizations try to hire them away from their present position by offering them increased benefits."

"Thank you," stated Professor Kelly. "Without a doubt, professionals tend to have excellent job security as their reputation grows. Their organization usually appreciates their efforts and professionalism and rewards them in any number of ways. As usual, you did an excellent job of coming up with a list of benefits related to our topic of discussion. Before we move on to the second half of this evening's session, take a few minutes to review the list of benefits you shared that relate to being professional." As the students analyzed the items on the board, this is what they saw.

BENEFITS OF BEING PROFESSIONAL

- Significantly increases the respect received.
- Enhances your self-confidence.
- Results in continuous improvement.
- Helps you remain calm in pressure situations.
- Tends to have excellent personal appearance.
- Enhances your productivity.
- Provides an excellent role model.
- Tends to perform best in key situations.
- Has excellent job security.

Professor Kelly said, "It's time to begin the second half of this evening's session. We have already determined that being professional is beneficial in many ways. We must now identify specific behaviors and actions exhibited by professionals. Who would like to begin?"

The student who was a realtor commented, "I believe that something that distinguishes one as being professional is that he or she lives and works according to priorities."

"Thank you very much," affirmed Dr. Kelly. "I agree that a professional lives and works according to priorities. We all know that most people are so busy that they cannot do everything they would like to. What we can do is focus our time and energy on high priorities. If we accomplish our high priorities, we can truly say that we have lived a successful life. Who has another idea to share?"

The student who was an executive suggested, "Professionals are those who continuously seek to better themselves. While they may already be regarded as successful, they strive to improve, especially in high-priority areas of their life and career."

"Thank you," said Dr. Kelly. "A trademark of highly successful individuals, those we can truly call professional, is that they strive to better themselves, whether it is through reading, attending seminars, or taking college classes like Leadership 101. As no one ever attains perfection, continuous improvement is something that we can strive for throughout our lives. Who else has an idea they would like to share?"

The student who was a lawyer said, "A professional tends to have excellent personal appearance and hygiene. As we stated earlier in the evening, the type of appearance that is appropriate varies from position to position, but professionals look appropriate for whatever career they happen to be in."

"Thank you," concurred Professor Kelly. "No matter what career area we are in, our appearance affects us in that others judge us by the way we look. Good grooming and a proper wardrobe create a definite impression on others and often affect the way we feel about ourselves. While I feel very comfortable in shorts and sweatshirts at home, I would not feel at ease if I wore such items when teaching or serving as a business consultant. Does someone else have an idea to share?"

The student who was a middle manager commented, "As a leader, a true professional corrects those whom he or she leads in private. It is never a good idea to criticize an employee in front of fellow employees or customers."

"Thank you," responded Dr. Kelly. "No one wants to be reprimanded in front of others. The professional selects the appropriate time and place to discuss privately the areas where the individual needs to improve. Who else has an idea to review with the class?"

The student who was an electrician said, "I believe true professionals complete their tasks on time. If I tell one of my customers that I will complete a job by noon, I always try to finish on time or even a little early."

"Thank you very much," said Dr. Kelly. "By completing our tasks on schedule, we show others that we value their time. While delays occur from time to time, we must realize that we complicate the lives of others when we finish our assignments later than scheduled. By finishing our tasks early or arriving for appointments a few minutes ahead of schedule, we enhance our reputation as a professional. Who has another idea to share?"

The student who was a human resource manager suggested, "A characteristic of many professionals is an extensive vocabulary. When I am interviewing individuals, one of the first things I notice is their language skills. Whether our employees are on the phone, writing a letter, or meeting personally with a client, having an adequate vocabulary is beneficial."

"Thank you," declared Professor Kelly. "Earlier we suggested that our appearance makes an impression on others. Similarly, our communication skills also influence the ways others perceive us. Reading regularly and using a dictionary when we come across words we do not understand can enhance our vocabulary in a relatively short period of time. Does someone else have an idea to share with the class?"

The student who was the manager of a department store commented, "Often professionals keep a record of their successes and failures as a way to improve further their abilities."

"Thank you," replied Dr. Kelly. "One such technique is keeping a journal of such positive and negative experiences. Through a journal a true professional continuously improves in priority areas, whether at work or in his or her personal life. In the journal the professional makes specific notes regarding the reasons why he or she was successful or failed in a particular aspect of his or her career or life. Scientists have been using what they call the scientific method for years. A journal allows the professional to similarly analyze his or her experiences. Who has another idea to express?"

The student who was a retiree said, "Individuals who are professional tend to seek out answers and opportunities rather than waiting for such information."

"Thank you very much," agreed Dr. Kelly. "Earlier in the Leadership 101 class, we discussed the importance of being 'action-minded,' seeking out ideas from others rather than waiting for others to come to us. Professionals are very active- minded and thus gain information and ideas at a much faster rate than others. Does anyone else have an idea to share?"

The student who was a doctor remarked, "Professional individuals are tactful in their remarks to others. One of my least favorite tasks is to inform a patient that he or she has a serious health problem. While this is something that must be done, I always try to imagine how I would want this information presented to me. I also try to provide some encouragement to my patient in these situations."

"Thank you very much," acknowledged Dr. Kelly. "Most of us face situations where being tactful is required. As the doctor pointed out, by thinking things through before speaking, we have taken a significant step in our attempt to be tactful towards others. Who else has an idea that they would like to share this evening?"

The student who was a waitress commented, "One of the characteristics of professionals is that they do not show favoritism. I have worked in a number of restaurants where people were favored because they were either related to or good friends with the owner or manager. This always created morale problems. It's best to treat everyone the same."

"Thank you," responded Professor Kelly. "While it is easy to like some people better than others, it is important not to show favoritism as we go about our work. By treating everyone well and not showing favoritism, we gain the respect of those we associate with. Does someone have another idea to share?"

The student who was a computer software specialist said, "Earlier we discussed how an extensive vocabulary can enhance our image. On the other hand, some individuals use inappropriate language and tarnish their reputation."

"Thank you very much," said Dr. Kelly. "While I have heard foul language used in a wide range of places, the use of such words lessens the image of its user. We should strive to avoid such language in all aspects of our lives, for the use of these words can become habit-forming and hard to break like any such bad habit. Are there any other ideas left to share?"

The student who was a pastor remarked, "I believe that a professional typically treats others with respect."

"Thank you very much," agreed Professor Kelly. "Often professionals treat everyone with the same respect often reserved for people in powerful positions. This is one of the important ways professionals can have a positive impact on the lives of others. Sometimes all others need is to be shown a little respect to help them move in a positive direction. Does someone else have an idea to share?"

The full-time college student said, "I believe that most professionals are enthusiastic about their careers. It's not a chore to them but an honor to go about their day-to-day activities."

"Thank you," remarked Dr. Kelly. "Being a professional is not simply attaining the degrees or awards that allow one to attain a fancy title. One becomes a true professional over the years as he or she conducts business in a competent and enthusiastic manner. We have time for one final idea to be shared in the Leadership 101 class. Does someone have one more trademark of a professional to share with the class?"

The student who was an accountant said, "One of the primary characteristics of a true professional is that he or she is consistent over the years."

"Thank you very much," replied Professor Kelly. "How many singers or groups have had one big hit and were never heard from again? How many professional baseball players had one good season and then spent the rest of their careers in the minor leagues? Consistency may be one of the most important indicators of professionalism. To attain the status of being a professional, one must consistently demonstrate the excellence that professionals are known for in all career areas. As has been suggested this evening, to attain this consistency requires a lot of hard work, reflection, and a constant search for ways to improve. The hard work pays off though, for those individuals are regarded as professionals."

"Well, that's it everyone. Thank you for making this such an outstanding Leadership 101 class. I hope that we all reap the benefits from the multitude of ideas that have been presented throughout the semester. I can't thank you enough for your dedication and hard work. You have made this a memorable experience for me, and I hope you feel the same."

The applause from the students brought a smile to Professor Kelly's face. He remarked, "Thank you again. Before leaving for the final time, please review the list of behaviors and actions that can be attributed to a professional." As the students reviewed the items on the board, this is what they observed.

BEHAVIORS / ACTIONS OF PROFESSIONALS

- They live and work according to priorities.
- They continuously seek to better themselves.
- They have excellent / appropriate appearance.
- They discipline others only in private.
- They complete tasks early or on time.
- They utilize an extensive vocabulary.
- They utilize a journal to analyze experiences.
- They are active-minded, seeking out ideas.
- They are tactful in their remarks to others.
- They treat everyone well . . . do not play favorites.
- They avoid foul language.
- They treat everyone with respect.
- They are enthusiastic about their career.
- They do excellent work on a consistent basis.

THE PROFESSIONAL
by Dr. Thomas J. Shaughnessy
AUGUST 30, 1998

The respect received is tremendous for the professional persons.
Self-confidence comes from all the practice and rehearsing.
Continuous improvement results and how they handle the pressure.
Appearance and productivity are two ways by which they are measured.

The success of the professionals provides an excellent role model for all
As they perform best in key situations, not likely to stumble or fall.
This earns them excellent job security as their employers are pleased
As they watch them live and work according to priorities.

As they seek ways to improve how they work in a flurry,
They get their tasks completed on time and quite often finish early.
Quite effective communicators, you'll not hear them swear.
I guess you might say, professionals are way above fair.

Daily they utilize a journal as they search for the reasons.
They continue to find success, season after season.
They are active-minded as they seek out the solutions
And are tactful and respectful, making many contributions.

They treat everyone well and are truly sincere
And avoid foul language, both in life and career.
Their enthusiasm shines forth, for they love what they do.
The professional is consistent and excels the whole year through.

ABOUT THE AUTHOR

Dr. Thomas J. Shaughnessy received his doctorate at the University of Illinois, Champaign-Urbana. He is professor of management, human relations, and business interns at Illinois Central College. Dr. Shaughnessy also teaches for the University of Illinois, Springfield Campus, Peoria Center.

Dr. Shaughnessy has won the *Gallion Award* at Illinois Central College, an award given to the faculty member students select as the teacher of the year. Dr. Shaughnessy has also done consulting work for both large corporations and small businesses. Dr. Shaughnessy's mission is to help both individuals and organizations attain a high level of success.

ADDITIONAL PROGRAMS CREATED BY DR. THOMAS J. SHAUGHNESSY.
Effective Leadership: The Foundation
Effective Leadership: The Traits, Benefits, Behaviors and Actions
Reflections on Success

SURVEY INSTRUMENTS
Job-related Factor Items: The Importance of Various Items.
Job-related Factor Items: Your Current Level of Satisfaction

The survey instruments are designed to allow an organization to determine:
1. Which job-related factor items are most important to their employees.
2. The current level of satisfaction each employee feels regarding individual job-related factor items.

By utilizing the survey instruments organizations should be able to both:
1. Reduce employee turnover.
2. Improve employee morale.

FOR ADDITIONAL INFORMATION
Dr. Thomas J. Shaughnessy
Illinois Central College
Room 334B
One College Drive, East Peoria, IL 61635
(309) 694-8433